MOOCs: Opportunities, Impacts, and Challenges

Massive Open Online Courses in Colleges and Universities

By Michael Nanfito

with contributions from Joey King, Sean Andrews, Georgianne Hewett, and Bryan Alexander

MOOCs: Opportunities, Impacts, and Challenges

Massive Open Online Courses in Colleges and Universities

By Michael Nanfito

with contributions from Joey King, Sean Andrews, Georgianne Hewett, and Bryan Alexander

Acknowledgments

Many individuals have contributed both directly and indirectly to this effort. I specifically want to thank Dr. Sean Andrews for his contributions to Chapter 1, *Isolating the Hype* and Georgianne Hewett for her insights and contributions to Chapter 2, *Identifying Expectation and Hope.* The research and presentations of Dr. Bryan Alexander serve to illuminate much of the analysis of trends in education and Dr. W. Joseph King has been instrumental in developing the approach to the larger issues addressed here. Finally, this would never have been possible without the editorial assistance, encouragement, and patience of Fred Moody.

Contents

Foreword

It's worth reviewing the MOOC landscape now that the dust has settled, or at least stopped blowing furiously and to reflect on the opportunities and challenges these iterative learning environments represent. The purpose in writing this survey is to give college and university leadership and governing boards, as well as faculty and staff, a thorough overview of the MOOC landscape in the hopes that it will help them knowledgably assess its opportunities and challenges. MOOCs and their associated technologies may indeed provide opportunities for higher education. But MOOC-related decisions need to be based on a mission-driven process that properly engages the entire institutional community. Only with such careful assessment can MOOC offerings be made a proper core component of your overall institutional venture.

The question that schools, colleges, and universities face relates to the educational institution's reason for being: How will tools like MOOCs further the mission of the institution? For institutions that traditionally have large, lecture-hall-based classes, or for whom distance learning is already a component of their core curriculum, a MOOC might simply be an extension in scale of those paradigms. For institutions that traditionally have small classes, or who have not embraced distance learning, the role of the MOOC and its component technologies is less clear. Whatever the case, the mission of the institution must drive the development of strategy and subsequent planning and decision-making.

As of this writing (October, 2013), there continues to be disagreement and confusion about the disposition of MOOCs. Some of the experiments that received very public pronouncements (Udacity and San Jose State for example) have dimmed if not gone dark, at least for now. MOOC advocates and opponents have strong views that, while ostensibly intended to clarify, have tended instead to obscure the range of issues campus leaders and program managers must grapple with as they identify next steps in addressing the review and possible implementation of MOOCs. This book attempts to help readers to identify, define, and challenge those assumptions.

This is not a scholarly argument on pedagogy and learning theory in online environments. Rather, it is intended to be a practical survey of a contemporary issue in higher education. An initiative as controversial and potentially divisive as MOOCs requires an inclusive, pan-institutional approach to investigation, review, planning, and implementation. Campus leadership is encouraged to develop a strong—and inclusive—program of planning to ensure that their institution is ready to appropriately integrate online learning.

Many institutions face daunting challenges with the development and implementation of MOOCs. The objective with this book is to help campus leaders make the best decisions for their institutions. Technology, support, funding, and organizational development are all concerns that must be part of the discussion if campus leadership is to actively manage online learning rather than blindly react to external pressures. To diminish or conceal the challenges would be ill advised at best. They are shared here to encourage and facilitate productive and challenging conversations on campuses across the country. Individuals strongly for or against MOOCs might perceive this process as unduly slow, but experience indicates otherwise.

Michael Nanfito

Technology vendors are changing rapidly so institutions require exceptional internal clarity as they decide on MOOCs, if only to ensure that they are not left holding the bag on vendor contracts. While many schools will make the conscious decision *not* to implement massive online learning programs, there is real value in making use of MOOCs in all their iterations as part of innovative and authentic efforts to engage in inter-institutional and international education.

We are currently caught up in a volatile, exciting time bereft of solid research into the pedagogy of online learning. The hope is that this book will be one of the agents encouraging support and development of that research. This is precisely why it focuses on the need for campus leadership to use this tumultuous time to its strategic advantage and forge effective internal programs and external partnerships in the course of its planning. Unlike other books attempting to document the history of online learning or the failure of the academy in the twenty-first century, this survey is intended to be a guide for individuals charged with making careful decisions in the face of persistent pressure (from faculty, staff, presidents, and trustees) to reflexively implement MOOCs *now*. These decision-makers are in both an unfortunate and an exciting position. The work they are doing, the decisions they are making, their responses to government legislation and mandates, will have profound impact on the nature of online education.

Recent surveys by Babson and others reveal mixed understanding and apprehension of MOOCs in every sector of higher education. Data and commentary from private and public, baccalaureate and doctoral, community-college and four-year institutions all reveal deep differences amongst campus leaders on what to do about online learning in general and MOOCs in particular. With this book, we strive to provide helpful prompts to individuals in every sector who are clamoring for more effective information to help them make the best decisions for their institutions. Presidents, trustees, provosts, librarians, faculty, and technologists will benefit from clear questions to ask and a concise analysis of the environment to employ on campus as they map their next steps.

Whatever decision a college or university makes regarding MOOCs, success will depend more upon institutional mission and a solid strategy than on first-to-market advantage. Indeed, the "market" is a great unknown. For all of the excitement about MOOCs, revenues—or even a revenue model—has been slow in coming. To date, MOOC providers have offered over a dozen ideas as to how revenue may be generated for their partner institutions, yet it remains theoretical at best, hypothetical at worst.

Given the unknown revenue potential and significant costs of MOOCs, it would behoove governing boards and institutional leadership to fully engage the institutional community through the normal mechanisms of shared governance. While these processes can be maddeningly slow, they are specifically designed to make difficult, mission-based decisions. The pace of the process also allows leadership to fully develop an associated strategy and plan for following through on a decision, and allows time to consider the implications of different revenue models.

Michael Nanfito

Part 1: The Landscape

Chapter 1: **Isolating the Hype**

Welcome to the college education revolution. Big breakthroughs happen when what is suddenly possible meets what is desperately necessary.[1] —Thomas Friedman

The story became legend almost immediately: In 2011, Stanford professor Sebastian Thrun and Peter Norvig, director of research at Google, decided to teach the course "Introduction to Artificial Intelligence" online, and make it available for free to anyone in the world with an Internet connection. 160,000 students enrolled and 20,000 completed the course. Within weeks of the conclusion of his class, Thrun resigned his tenure-track position and founded Udacity, a for-profit provider of "massive open online courses," or MOOCs, with substantial investment from the VC firm Charles River Ventures. Thrun's stated objective was to have 500,000 students in his first Udacity class.

There followed an immediate flurry of announcements of new startups offering free access to MOOCs. Thrun's Stanford colleagues Daphne Koller and Andrew Ng launched their own startup, Coursera, announcing that they would offer fourteen classes beginning in February and March 2012. Professors from Stanford, the University of Michigan at Ann Arbor, and the University of California at Berkeley would teach the courses. Not to be outdone, MIT launched MITx, built upon its popular Open Courseware system. That effort quickly blossomed into edX, a non-profit partnership between MIT and Harvard, with each school contributing a combined $60 million to build what Harvard's announcement billed as "the single biggest change in education since the printing press."

This spike in startups prompted *New York Times* columnist Thomas Friedman to declare it "a college education revolution." The *Wall Street Journal* similarly declared that the "nation, and the world, are in the early stages of a historic transformation in how students learn, teachers teach, and schools and school systems are organized."

And with that—in a matter of a few months—MOOCs became the topic of the year in higher education.

The press coverage was not lost on college and university presidents and trustees around the country. Institutions faced increasing pressure to board the MOOC bandwagon with little regard for the actual value of MOOCs. Most infamously, The University of Virginia Board of Visitors (temporarily) fired its president for adhering to a thoughtful program of "incremental, marginal change," in the regents' words, rather than participating in the coming MOOC "transformation… legitimized by some of the elite institutions" in the nation. (The president was reinstated after a highly publicized, campus-wide protest by faculty and students.)

Despite rumblings about the lack of a sound business plan for MOOCS, their massive dropout rates, and the lack of college credit for participation, the proclamations kept piling up.

MOOCs Threaten the Traditional Business Model of Higher Education. In a June 2012 interview with the *Chronicle of Higher Education*, Bill Gates suggested that the ideal modification of the credential system would involve disconnecting representation of the range of an individual's knowledge from the current metric of college degrees conferred. (Gates himself has a high school diploma and makes substantial use of available resources to deepen his personal knowledge.) He noted that MOOCs and changes in credentialing are a valuable step in aligning educational infrastructure with employment and business needs. The following September, the Bill and Melinda Gates Foundation announced that it would award ten grants of up to $50,000 each for MOOCs offering "high-enrollment, low-success introductory-level courses." That same month, Stanford appointed John C. Mitchell, professor of computer science at the university, as vice provost for online learning, the first new such position in twenty years. Days later, Moody's Investors Service released the report, "*Shifting Ground: Technology Begins to Alter Centuries-Old Business Model for Universities.*" The report further inflamed media frenzy by declaring that MOOCs may elevate the financial stature of elite institutions while simultaneously increasing financial challenges to less-wealthy institutions.

As colleges and universities grappled with constant pronouncements that MOOCs will either save them or challenge them, publishers saw potential profit in the rise and delivery of massive online courses. MIT Press director Ellen W. Faran announced that the Press was "actively tracking the development of MOOCs and believe they do represent a promising market for university-press titles." The trend seemed to lend weight to some of the strategies of startups like Flat World Knowledge, a textbook publisher experimenting with business and pricing models. Flat World Knowledge was advertising its innovative business model as "free online and affordable offline." (However, in November 2012, citing financial concerns, the company announced that it was forced to drop free access.)

The MOOC wave rolled on. By fall 2012, Coursera had doubled its number of participating institutions, Wesleyan University had become the first liberal arts college on Coursera's roster (one of its courses was taught by the school's president), and Colorado State University became the first school to offer brick-and-mortar credits for MOOC course completion. By the end of 2012, Wellesley, UC Berkeley, and the University of Texas system were all working with edX, 100,000 students were taking Harvard's edX classes, there were two million registered Coursera students, and the American Council on Education (ACE) had committed to reviewing designated MOOCs for the purpose of certifying them for transferrable course credit.

The portrayal and reception of MOOCs, intentional or not, as an inspired innovation springing from the heads of a few talented and clearly brilliant educators and entrepreneurs brought on a rash of highly publicized expectations and concerns. Proponents cited MOOCs as a solution to the current crisis in higher education, with its ever-rising costs and ever-lessening value to newly minted graduates entering the job market. Detractors eyed them as destroyers of institutions delivering an invaluable higher-education experience made up of face-to-face instruction and the ineffable benefits of living and learning in a campus community. Reaction on both (or all) sides of the issue has been disproportionate, characterized by considerably more heat than light.

From the early days of the new "revolution," although reasonable people tried to articulate both the values and challenges MOOCs might offer, their questions tended to be drowned out by the volume of heated argument. Yet the questions remain viable: Why would colleges grant course credit to students who take MOOCs without paying tuition? How would an institution evaluate MOOC credits on the transcripts of students applying for admission? Are MOOCs even sustainable? What is the actual cost of hosting and delivering them? How will we balance support needs for existing programs with the potential that MOOCS represent? What exactly is their inherent value to both institutions and students?

Conversation about MOOCs now gives way to more thoughtful reflection and recollection. The idea that MOOCs are profoundly "disruptive" to the traditional paradigm for higher education echoes pronouncements about earlier technological innovations. The telegraph, for example, was declared a world changing "instantaneous highway of thought"; the radio, "the University of the Air" that would eliminate the need for physical attendance at institutions of higher learning. In 1961, Buckminster Fuller, in his essay *Education Automation*, described his vision for massive and individualized learning systems, predicting that nothing would be "quite so surprising or abrupt in the history of man as the forward evolution in the educational processes."

There is a conventional picture or concept of school that is very powerful in most men's minds, and I think a great surprise is coming. I don't think that what is going to happen in education is apprehended or anticipated at all by the political states. I know that there is awareness of coming change amongst the forward thinkers of the educational ranks, but, I feel, even they will be astonished at the magnitude of the transformation about to take place in the educational processes.

Similarly, in his 1962 *Augmenting Human Intellect: A Conceptual Framework*, Douglas Engelbart developed and proposed a new research agenda to the Stanford Research Institute, emphasizing the potential of computers for extending the human intellect. More recently, during the dot.com bubble of the 1990s, colleges and universities wrestled with the need to be online and embrace and integrate the new World Wide Web.

Seen in the light of this history, the breathless pronouncements that MOOCs are world changing can seem silly at best. But MOOCs should also be viewed not as overhyped, unprecedented, and revolutionary developments so much as nodes in a decades-long trajectory of innovation in learning and open education resources. MOOCs were not invented out of whole cloth; rather, they are built upon previous, less-publicized breakthroughs in online learning and open educational resources, and thus are an incremental step forward in the movement toward delivering education online:

Since its founding Sloan-C has evolved into "an institutional and professional leadership organization dedicated to integrating online education into the mainstream of higher education, helping institutions and individual educators improve the quality, scale, and breadth of online education." As a direct of result of the Foundation's investments several significant online learning programs have been implemented, including The University of Maryland University College, Penn State World Campus, and the UMASS Online Learning Network. In addition, the State University of New York (SUNY), the University of Central Florida and other large state university systems have developed online learning programs. Many institutions and individuals have been at this for a long

Michael Nanfito

while and in November of 2012 Sloan-C held their 18th Annual International Conference on Online Learning.

At the conference Jack Wilson, president emeritus of the University of Massachusetts who also founded UMass Online in 2001, offered remarks that gave voice to the irritation some online learning veterans felt in the wake of media reports about the upstart MOOC startups. Some of these veterans' irritations bubbled to the surface as a result of remarks that MOOCs might replace all other forms of online learning and maybe even traditional higher education itself. Many expressed concern that the recent involvement of high profile, high-risk startups and elite colleges would diminish the work of agencies already in the field. "They're certainly not the first movers; they're not even the fast followers," Wilson said. "It's great to have them on board. But that is not who has led online learning, or who is going to lead online learning." Sebastian Thrun presented a keynote address at the conference. His comments illustrated the chasm between the veterans and the newcomers when he acknowledged to those present that he was "pretty much ignorant of your work" when he began to conceive of what since became the commercial MOOC provider Udacity.

If MOOCs are to be as influential and ubiquitous as many predict, the effort of colleges and universities (and organizations and associations) not on the roster of elite campuses must be acknowledged and supported. Here is a brief enumeration of less well-known MOOC predecessors:

> **Fathom**. In the late 1990s, Columbia University established Fathom as a for-profit effort to leverage the Web as a strategic resource for extending higher education's reach to a public hungry for access to

educational resources. Ann Kirschner, now Dean of Macaulay Honors College at The City University of New York, was retained to develop the program. Kirschner architected Fathom as an online learning community of practice for public audiences interested in the experience of "being at a great university or a great museum." Regarding Fathom and its place in the developmental trajectory of online learning, Kirschner noted that "learning is not limited to the classroom, and the many other types of content provided through Fathom will provide a more complete and accessible context for knowledge. We believe that Fathom will define the transformation of the online learning category into a broader interactive knowledge marketplace." Columbia invested $25 million in the venture, and 65,000 people created accounts, but few participants paid for any of the courses and the effort failed to turn a profit. Columbia closed Fathom in 2003, retaining the site's online content until mid-2011.

Sunoikisis. Sunoikisis is a national consortium of Classics programs that began in 2000 as an initiative of the Associated Colleges of the South (ACS). Sunoikisis provides inter-institutional courses for students of the Classics. Since its beginning, it has demonstrated how to leverage technology to create extended curricular offerings across multiple campuses. The Sunoikisis program offers a wider range of disciplinary coursework, interaction with student peers and faculty than would ever be possible at a single small liberal arts college. Faculty and students from thirty-five colleges have participated in Sunoikisis programs since its inception.

Connexions. "Connexions," its web site declares, "is a dynamic digital educational ecosystem consisting of an educational content repository and a content management system optimized for the delivery of educational content." Connexions was launched as a non-profit start-up by Rice University in 1999, with the explicit aim to "reinvent how we write, edit, publish, and use textbooks and other learning materials." Connexions is a repository of open educational resources that can be described in four words that borrow from an Apple advertising slogan and a book by Lawrence Lessig:

Create – in Connexions, everyone is free to create educational materials and contribute them to the repository;

Rip – in Connexions, everyone is free to copy the material and customize it;

Mix – in Connexions, everyone is free to mix the material together into new books and courses;

Burn – in Connexions, everyone is free to create finished products like e-learning web courses, CD-ROMs, and even printed books.

NOTE: Although Fathom was discontinued a decade ago, both Sunoikisis and Connexions remain active.

These are but three examples of projects and programs that represent significant components in the development of online learning. MOOCs are the most recent and most heavily publicized, and are themselves evolving. Ultimately, each generation's wave of hyped arguments promoting the disruptive nature of technological progress necessarily matures, growing from provocative visions of Apocalypse or Paradise into a more prosaic real-world application

Today, confronted with various "flavors" of MOOC, we have the opportunity and obligation to determine exactly how they make sense for higher education, and to recognize that they are here to stay in some form. It may be that MOOCs will eventually play a broader social, economic, and cultural role than one that is higher-education-specific. Whatever the case, we in higher education must take this opportunity to examine how MOOCs might fit into the broader context of twenty-first-century higher education— an exercise requiring not that we assess MOOCs in and of themselves, but that we assess how they can be made a meaningful part of an institution's overall strategy.

Chapter 1: Endnotes

1. Friedman, "Come the Revolution."

Michael Nanfito

Chapter 1: Isolating the Hype - Recommended Readings

Azevedo, Alisha. "In Colleges' Rush to Try MOOC's, Faculty Are Not Always in the Conversation." *The Chronicle of Higher Education*, September 26, 2012, sec. Technology.

"Columbia Digital -- Fathom Disseminates Knowledge from Columbia and Other Members of the Fathom Consortium to a Global Audience." *Columbia Digital*.

Davidson, Cathy. "If We Profs Don't Reform Higher Ed, We'll Be Re-Formed (and We Won't Like It)." *HASTAC*, January 13, 2013.

Engelbart, Douglas C. "Augmenting Human Intellect: A Conceptual Framework - 1962 (AUGMENT,3906,) - Doug Engelbart Institute," October 1962.

Fain, Paul. "ACE to Assess Udacity Courses for Credit." *Inside Higher Ed*, January 16, 2013.

Fain, Paul, and Ry Rivard. "California Bill to Encourage MOOC Credit at Public Colleges | Inside Higher Ed." *Inside Higher Ed*, March 13, 2013.

Friedman, Thomas L. "Come the Revolution." *The New York Times*, May 15, 2012, sec. Opinion.

Fuller, R. Buckminster. *Education Automation: Comprehensive Learning for Emergent Humanity*. Edited by Jaime Snyder. 1st ed. Lars Müller Publishers, 2009.

Howard, Jennifer. "Publishers See Online Mega-Courses as Opportunity to Sell Textbooks." *The Chronicle of Higher Education*, September 17, 2012, sec. Technology.

Lederman, Doug. "ACE Deems 5 Massive Open Courses Worthy of Credit." *Inside Higher Ed*, February 7, 2013.

Mangan, Katherine. "Gates Foundation Offers Grants for MOOC's in Introductory Classes." The Chronicle of Higher Education. *The Wired Campus*, September 11, 2012.

"Moody's: 2013 Outlook for Entire US Higher Education Sector Changed to Negative." *Moody's Investors Service*, January 16, 2013.

Nikias, C. L. Max. "Online Education—Hype and Reality," August 27, 2012.

Rivard, Ry. "California Academic Leaders Oppose Outsourcing Plan." *Inside Higher Ed*, March 28, 2013.

Young, Jeffrey R. "A Conversation With Bill Gates About the Future of Higher Education." *The Chronicle of Higher Education*, June 25, 2012, sec. Technology.

———. "At Conference, Leaders of 'Traditional' Online Learning Meet Upstart Free Providers." The Chronicle of Higher Education. *The Wired Campus*, October 11, 2012.

———. *Bill Gates on: The Meaning of MOOC's*, 2012. http://vimeo.com/47732039.

Chapter 2: Identifying Expectation and Hope

"MOOCs have the potential (if we do it well) for making higher education available globally to those who cannot afford it. In this particular sense, MOOCs are not a threat to conventional U.S. brick-and-mortar education. They offer a form of education to those for whom education is off limits."[2]
—Cathy Davidson

In general, people are fascinated with trends that predict dramatic changes in the way we live, work, communicate and learn. Whether The Next Big Thing" or "The End of [insert established cultural milieu here] As We Know It," trends that have the potential to deconstruct the familiar seduce us into obsessing about them and endlessly bandying them about in conversation and debate. We relish in reacting—often with little information—to evolutions (and advertised revolutions) that promise to move us further from how it was done in our day.

That has certainly been the case with MOOCs. In late 2011 and early 2012, anyone following education media might have seen them mentioned in one or two articles each week. But before the year was out, MOOCs had come to dominate education news and draw crowds to conferences and online webinars. Now, hopes for MOOCs have blown sky-high. But what exactly do we hope to gain from this latest iteration of online learning? What actual problems are MOOCs expected to solve? Reading the plethora of essays, articles, blog posts, and survey results on the topic makes clear that expectations for MOOCs are varied and contradictory.

A quick survey of publicly declared hopes reveals that MOOCs will reduce the cost of education, increase the cost of education, save money, make money, lower tuition, raise tuition, generate revenue, incur additional costs, shorten time to graduation, increase enrollments, ensure that students are able to register for required courses, provide data for learning analytics, kick-start competency-based assessment programs, provide the highest quality education from the most elite institutions for free, and solve the global education crisis.

Each of these expectations has been expressed in serious articles and essays this past year. But those who have stripped away the Next-Big-Thing veneer from the MOOC debate have begun to understand that MOOCs *can* be made a useful tool for higher education. MOOCs in all of their manifestations can connect learners, instructors, and knowledge in dynamic and extensible ways. They can foster student-centered learning and require students to take responsibility for their education in a forthright manner.

For those charged with defining the strategic direction of institutions of higher education, however, it is vital to guard against being swept up in the wave of overheated rhetoric and keep a focus on strategies that advance the institutional mission. Carefully analyze reports and review them with staff and colleagues in the context of your stated strategic plan. And in the review and analysis of potential MOOCs, keep in mind the role that learning plays in modern life generally. Such an exercise provides a baseline for productive review.

We are hard-wired to learn from the moment we are born. Whether we attended public or private school, were

Michael Nanfito

home-schooled, or fall into the newer category of the "unschooled," we are all learners. We are excited by the discovery of subjects that capture our interest and stir our imagination. We value lessons that expand our knowledge, change our perspective and send us down new paths. We disdain work or education requirements that chafe and feel like a waste of time. At its core—and most pertinent to the present conversation about MOOCs—learning connects us to one another. This is why MOOCs are so inherently appealing at first glance: they promise to deliver access to learning and interaction in a new, almost infinitely expansive mode. If we regard MOOCs in the broader context of our regard for learning, we are better positioned to discern their inherent potential and the role they could play as part of an institution's strategic mission.

Campus Leaders reveal their hopes and expectations. In an interview with the Wall Street Journal John Hennessy, President of Stanford revealed his anticipation for the future: "What I told my colleagues is there's a tsunami coming. I can't tell you exactly how it's going to break, but my goal is to try to surf it, not to just stand there." There is clearly value in identifying the hopes and expectations we have for MOOCs, online learning, and open education resources. (It is requisite that we analyze MOOCs not as a standalone construct but in the larger context of the development of all open and online education resources.) There is now a substantial, representative body of work to review that can help us understand the thinking of presidents, provosts, and other academic leaders in regard to the immediate and future potential of these emerging technologies.

In 2011, as we began to hear a bit more about MOOCs,

Kenneth C. (Casey) Green conducted a "Presidential Perspectives" survey of nine hundred fifty-six campus and university system presidents and chancellors for *Inside Higher Ed.* The results include the following:

- A majority of presidents believe that online education supports the mission of their institution and provides an opportunity to increase tuition revenues.

- Seventy-eight percent of presidents surveyed believe that online learning provides a vehicle to reach more learners and thus increase enrollment.

- The percentage of presidents who believe online education is a means to increase enrollment and revenue was "consistently high across all sectors, although slightly higher among public institutions than independent institutions and highest in community colleges."

Elsewhere in 2011, fifty-seven percent of academic leaders reported that open education resources would have *value* for their campus (less than five percent disagreed), and nearly two-thirds of all chief academic officers agreed that open education resources offer the potential to reduce costs for their institution. There was wide agreement among most academic leaders that this cost reduction would result from the impact that access to open education resources would have in the development of new courses in the curriculum. Yet only one-half of all chief academic officers report that any of the courses at their institution currently use OER materials.

In November 2012, the Babson Survey Research Group's survey *Growing the Curriculum: Open Education Resources in U.S. Higher Education* reported findings on the expectations of campus leaders on this issue. Many academic leaders were only minimally aware of the role of open education resources in higher education and just over half identified themselves as being "Aware" or "Very aware." Moreover, when explaining their understanding of open resources, most of these respondents equated "open" with "free." It is important to understand that there are costs related to the development of open resources. When your college or university contemplates this opportunity, consider the steps you and your staff will take to identify those costs in order to work towards a return on your investment. (This is a critical component of MOOCs that we will address at greater length in subsequent chapters.)

More recently, in January 2013, the Babson Survey Research Group's annual Survey of Online Learning was released. *Changing Course: Ten Years of Tracking Online Education in the United States* is the tenth annual report on the state of online learning in U.S. higher education. The survey asked a range of questions about institutional use of and plans for MOOCs, and the answers reveal a mixed bag of expectations.

Nearly seventy percent of chief academic leaders who responded believe that online learning will have a critical role in their long-term institutional strategy, while eleven percent do not. Twenty-seven percent of respondents said they don't believe MOOCs are a sustainable method for delivering courses, twenty-eight percent said they are, and thirty-five percent were neutral. Yet seventy-seven percent of chief academic officers rate the learning outcomes in online learning as "equal or superior to those in traditional face-to-face courses"—an increase from the fifty-seven percent who rated them as such when Babson first asked the question in 2003. Interestingly, while the majority of academic leaders remain unconvinced that MOOCs themselves represent a sustainable method for delivering online courses in the context of their institution, nearly sixty percent believe that MOOCs provide an important means to *learn about* online pedagogy. Also noteworthy: the percentage of chief academic officers who believe that faculty members on their campuses appreciate the value and legitimacy of online education is now thirty percent— *lower* than the results from the same question in 2004.

There is a general sense that access to open educational resources will benefit campuses. There is less specificity about what exactly the benefits are, or how they will manifest themselves. Kenneth Hartman, senior fellow at Edventures and the former president of Drexel eLearning at Drexel University, has recommendations that are worth review when working to identify institutional expectations for open resources and online learning. As Hartman suggests in his February 11, 2013 Insider Higher Ed article, *Tips for college leaders to make online programs work*, the "fundamental question that must first be addressed (and consciously built around) is 'Why are we doing e-learning?'" There are several possible reasons including the need to increase tuition revenue and decrease costs; create greater access and allow greater flexibility for students; experiment with pedagogical approaches to better educate a new generation of students.

Before considering the benefits of MOOCs and e-learning, it helps to decide what a "benefit" is in the larger institutional context. Identify institutional *expectations* and precisely synch them with institutional *needs*. Assess organizational structure and its capacity to meet expectations. As Hartman states, if you are new to the online learning space, "it requires the thoughtful

Michael Nanfito

use of both internal and external resources, including . . . the careful use of third-party vendors and consultants to properly assess your institution's market niche." Without knowing the "why," it makes no sense to press too far down the path toward the "how."

Beyond such obvious hopes and expectations as increasing tuition, raising revenue, and extending institutional brands, there are other provocative expectations that merit scrutiny, fueled by healthy skepticism. These are not necessarily the only expectations that MOOCs elicit, but they seem to resonate the most widely.

Equitable and expansive access. One of the more intriguing and marketable aspects of MOOCs is their potential for allowing all students to enroll in highly valued courses and study with distinguished faculty from the most elite schools in the world. This is built into the MOOC program offered by Coursera, for example, which is contractually limited to partnering with elite universities. This MOOC model affords unprecedented access to talented professors at prestigious universities.

Closely related to the potential of studying with prestigious faculty is the possibility of creating equitable, worldwide access to education. A new era of globalization is looming, and MOOCs may be a big part of it. American colleges and universities have long sought to bring a global perspective to their students, but they have done so in fairly traditional ways. Study abroad and international exchange programs are typically constrained by institutional, programmatic, and geographic boundaries (not to mention funding and support). By contrast, the vision of MOOCs convening cadres of students from all over the world to share diverse perspectives and learn from one another in a massive, open, and collegial space seems to offer great promise for education.

MOOCs, by definition and design, are available for free to anyone with the wherewithal to connect to the Internet. Although that is by no means a universal audience, the capacity to connect continues to increase. The rapid deployment of smart cell phones even in nations with rudimentary Internet access, and the concomitant re-development of web resources to be mobile-device compliant, further increases the potential reach of MOOCs.

As Duke University's Cathy Davidson says in "If We Profs Don't Reform Higher Ed, We'll Be Re-Formed (and we won't like it)," there are far too few colleges and universities and far too many students with academic aspirations for the current system to accommodate them all. In a world which increasingly clamors for an educated global populace with the critical analytical skills that college education provides, we are asking too much of the existing education infrastructure. MOOCs have the potential to address this burgeoning challenge.

In India, ninety-eight percent of the five hundred thousand hopefuls whose academic standing qualifies them to take the entrance exams to the Indian Institutes of Technology are rejected. Ironically, many of those rejected qualify them for their second choice: elite schools in the United States. Similarly, Peking University has a one-half of one percent acceptance rate, as compared with Harvard's nearly six percent acceptance rate.[3]

MOOCs can make an emerging form of higher education available to many who are excluded because of space limitations or inability to pay. Most of these potential

Michael Nanfito

students would never become a matriculated student on a college campus in the United States (or anywhere else, for that matter). As Davidson notes, MOOCs "offer a form of education to those for whom education is off limits." In MOOCs there lies hope for a system that has the capacity to connect elite educators with eager learners who have access to few—or no—alternatives.

Analytics, assessment, and improved educational outcomes. The massive nature of MOOCs offers a new laboratory for approaches to developing competency-based assessment. Many have longed for the opportunity to make use of emerging analytical tools in education. We have large amounts of data that is unstructured and lacks context. MOOCs are poised to provide purposeful data sets about student interaction with course materials. We may have a new opportunity to feed the analyses and make predictive decisions about performance and outcomes in those courses for which such an approach makes sense. In "Can Big Data Analytics Boost Graduation Rates," Ellis Booker noted that "the advent of computer-mediated and online instruction, especially massive open online courses (MOOCs) with their tens of thousands of students per class, are changing what's possible." MOOCs, as a result of their scale, "provide so much data about student interactions, not only with the course material but with teachers and even other students. This massive amount of data can be parsed, compared, merged, modeled and analyzed, with the goal of improving educational outcomes." Progress may well be made in the refinement of the analytics and development of data collection from MOOC environments. The application of these metrics to the data mined from MOOCs has the potential to teach us a great deal about learning in online environments.

Desire2Learn, a company that provides learning management systems to the education market, is investing big in big data. "In the last three or four years, we built a team of five PhDs who've built algorithms and models to predict student performance," says company CEO John Baker. The company created a "risk quadrant," a visual representation of how each student is likely to do in an online course. The predictions are made dynamically on a week-to-week basis. After launching a beta version of their analytics program, Baker noted that "depending on the availability of historical data associated with a specific course, we are able to achieve accuracy rates approaching ninety-five percent as early as week two or three." These results were validated with research data sets, including one from the University of Wisconsin. This research echoes some of the data received from surveys of chief academic officers who hope that MOOCs and other iterations of online learning will afford opportunities to learn more about best practices in online learning.

Reduce the cost and improve the access. For many, the value of MOOCs lies in their potential to reduce the cost of education and corresponding bottlenecks in course registrations. They hope that MOOCs will create increasingly accessible, low-cost paths for learners and reduce the overhead of developing and delivering courses. Clayton Christensen, in *The Innovative University*, profiled the success of BYU-Idaho in that college's development of an online program that simultaneously grew the student population while reducing cost. BYU-Idaho offers online degree programs for $65 per credit, reducing the cost of a degree to less than $10,000. Similarly, the University of Texas announced plans to explore the deployment of

MOOCs with the stated hope of reducing the cost of a UT degree for at least some students. The university has partnered with edX in hopes of using edX courses to get more students into the pipeline and through college more rapidly and for less money.

Students in the United States are increasingly shut out of courses, unable to register for required classes because of high demand and an overburdened infrastructure. Students who have already matriculated are increasingly placed on waiting lists for classes they need to complete their degrees, transfer to four-year institutions, or register for enough courses to remain qualified for financial aid. State colleges and universities in California, New York, and elsewhere look to MOOCs and other online learning models to open up access to required courses for students suffering from being stuck in systems that are increasingly unable to meet demand.

As our network connections grow and evolve, we begin to question the theory of Dunbar's number, that cognitive limit on the number of people with whom we can successfully sustain active and stable relationships. We find intriguing possibility and potential as we navigate new and existing relationships in the context of our layered network ties. The promise of active and intellectual engagement with innumerable minds is inspiring. MOOCs provide hope to connect in a structured manner and in new ways with individuals who share our interests and enthusiasms. MOOCs are open and inviting; at present, the only price of admission is curiosity and an Internet connection. MOOCs are not restricted to the traditional student—which makes the diversity of participants itself well worth reviewing, as we do in our next chapter.

Chapter 2 Endnotes

2. Davidson, "If We Profs Don't Reform Higher Ed, We'll Be Re-Formed (and We Won't Like It)."

3. Ibid.

Chapter 2: Identifying Expectation and Hope - Recommended Readings

Allen, I. Elaine, and Jeff Seaman. "Ten Years of Tracking Online Education in the United States." Babson Survey Research Group, January 2013.

Booker, Ellis. "Can Big Data Analytics Boost Graduation Rates?" *Information Week*, February 5, 2013.

Christensen, Clayton M., and Henry J. Eyring. *The Innovative University: Changing the DNA of Higher Education from the Inside Out*. 1st ed. Jossey-Bass, 2011.

Davidson, Cathy. "If We Profs Don't Reform Higher Ed, We'll Be Re-Formed (and We Won't Like It)." *HASTAC*, January 13, 2013.

Green, Kenneth C. "Mission, MOOCs, & Money." *Association of Governing Boards*, February 2013.

Hartman, Kenneth E. "Tips for College Leaders to Make Online Programs Work." *Inside Higher Ed*, February 11, 2013.

Mossberg, Walt. "Changing the Economics of Education." *Wall Street Journal*, June 4, 2012.

Pappano, Laura. "Massive Open Online Courses Are Multiplying at a Rapid Pace." *The New York Times*, November 2, 2012, sec. Education / Education Life.

Chapter 3: **The Demographics of MOOCs**

Things that can't last don't. This is why MOOCs matter. Not because distance learning is some big new thing or because online lectures are a solution to all our problems, but because they've come along at a time when students and parents are willing to ask themselves, "Isn't there some other way to do this?"[4] —Clay Shirkey, "How to Save College"

Ultimately, students are not concerned with the distinctions we make about online learning platforms. They look to those of us in higher education to provide an accessible environment in which they can excel and attain their academic objectives. MOOCs must be discussed, planned for, and implemented as an additive component in a broader online learning environment that provides flexibility and choice to students trying to navigate a higher education system in transition.

The 2013 Babson Survey, *Changing Course: Ten Years of Tracking Online Education in the United States*, confirmed that enrollments in online education are increasing (although retention and completion rates remain low) in the face of declining enrollment in higher education overall. This suggests that MOOCs can develop, even thrive, in the current environment.

An overview of current online learning helps contextualize MOOCs. Over 6.7 million—roughly one third—of all higher education students took at least one online course during the fall 2011 term. This was an increase of 570,000 students over the previous year and a noteworthy increase over 2002's 1.6 million. Thirty-two percent of higher education students now take at least one course online. More than 70 percent of public and for-profit colleges now offer online academic programs (as opposed to single courses). Roughly half of private nonprofit colleges now offer online programs—nearly double the number doing so in 2002. Other key findings from the report:

- 77 percent of academic leaders rate the learning outcomes in online education as the same or superior to those in face-to-face courses.

- Low completion rates are an obstacle for the growth of online learning.

- 88.8 percent of academic leaders surveyed believe that student discipline in online courses is a barrier to growth, and just over 40 percent believe the same is true regarding acceptance of online degrees by potential employers.

Online learning in all forms is expanding for several reasons, including the growing number of students unable to gain access to classrooms. Campuses are struggling to accommodate the needs of matriculated students unable to register for required classes, transfer to four-year colleges, or maintain eligibility for financial aid. As a result, more college and university systems across the country are considering MOOCs. In addition to hoping to alleviate enrollment issues, many are betting on MOOCs to generate new revenue, reduce the cost of education, decrease time to graduation, and maximize return on investment.

The following is a brief overview of how some state systems are integrating MOOCs into their online portfolios.

New York. In March 2013, the State University of New York's Board of Trustees announced support of a plan to use MOOCs, prior-learning assessment, and competency-based

　　　　　　Michael Nanfito

programs to increase enrollment, shorten time to completion for degrees, and reduce the cost of education. The SUNY board intends to leverage expansion of the current prior-learning assessment program of the system's Empire State College and will encourage more faculty to teach MOOCs so as to maximize return on that investment. There are one hundred fifty online degree programs offered across the system, developed, delivered, and administered by each individual campus. As part of an effort to reduce costs, create a three-year degree program, streamline administration, and expand curricular offerings to non-traditional students, SUNY Chancellor Nancy Zimpher intends to consolidate these online offerings. SUNY aims to increase enrollment by one hundred thousand students in three years.

Florida. Where the Chancellor's office is taking the lead in the New York system, Florida lawmakers tentatively plan to place a single university—likely the University of Florida—in charge of expanding online efforts while simultaneously streamlining administrative overhead and oversight. Florida's online offerings and administration currently are scattered across the system, with nearly three hundred ninety online degree programs offered by ten of its twelve schools. Each campus administers its own design, development, and delivery of online courses. If the proposed legislation passes, Florida's university system will offer two new undergraduate degree programs by January 2014 and four more in the following year, while consolidating authority and eliminating redundancies. Florida, like New York, intends to leverage existing programs and take advantage of MOOCs to reduce the cost of education and increase enrollment.

California. In California, where cutbacks in state support led to decrease in the number of available course sections just as student demand increased, the legislature is reviewing a bill to use MOOCs and online learning to solve their higher education woes. [As of this writing] Senate Bill 520, sponsored by State Senator Darrell Steinberg, calls for a system enabling students experiencing trouble registering for lower-level, high-demand classes to take approved online courses offered by commercial providers outside the state's higher-education system. If the bill is passed and signed into law by Governor Jerry Brown (in the face of strong opposition from faculty in all three California college systems), state colleges and universities may soon be accepting credits earned by students enrolled in MOOCs.

Enrollment and completion data. Higher education has invested in online course delivery for years, and the investment is increasing. Many colleges, universities, and state legislatures are well on their way to responding to enrollment problems with MOOCs. Given the pressure to leverage this solution, it is vital to understand who is actually taking MOOCs, identifying their motivations, participation, location and behavior, and sorting out the factors contributing to and discouraging their productive participation.

Because official statistics are not yet published for every MOOC, data is developmental. Phil Hill, an education technology consultant, and Katy Jordan, a Ph.D. student at Open University, have been actively researching, compiling, and publishing this data. Hill identifies five categories of MOOC participants and provides information on their behavior and activities:

No-Shows, who register but never log in to a course while it is active, appear to be the largest group of those registering for Coursera-style MOOCs.

Observers, who log in and may read content or browse discussions but do not take any form of assessment beyond pop-up quizzes embedded in videos.

Drop-Ins, perform some activity (watch videos, browse, or participate in a discussion forum) for a select topic within the course, but do not attempt to complete the entire course. Some of these students are focused participants who use MOOCs informally to find content that help them meet course goals elsewhere.

Passive Participants, who view a course as content to consume. They may watch videos, take quizzes, read discussion forums, but generally do not engage with the assignments.

Active Participants, who fully participate in the MOOC and take part in discussion forums, the majority of assignments and all quizzes and assessments.[5]

One hallmark of the discourse on MOOCs is the emphasis on numbers. Massive MOOC enrollment figures are reminiscent of the eyeballs-on-web-pages "metrics" of the 1990s dot.com boom in the way they are used to stir imagination and controversy, and raise money and expectations.

An impressive enrollment figure of one hundred eighty thousand is often cited as the largest MOOC ever. But an initial enrollment of fifty thousand is typical, as is a ninety percent dropout rate.

As Hill notes, most enrolled individuals do not participate beyond watching a video or two before abandoning the course by its second week. Jordan compiled a sampling of data from twenty-four MOOCs—nineteen from Coursera, three from edX, one from Udacity and one from MITx (precursor to edX)—concluding that a completion rate of less than ten percent is typical. The average completion rate of Coursera-style xMOOCs is 7.6 percent, with a minimum of 0.67 percent and a maximum of 19.2 percent.[6]

While comparing enrollment numbers to completion rates is eye-catching, the dramatic discrepancy between the two does not provide useful decision-making data for colleges and universities. It is not the best measure of MOOC engagement in the context of higher education, for one simple reason: MOOCs in their current iteration are not "college courses" in the traditional model, with prerequisites, tuition, textbook fees, and grades that lead to credit and credentials. Rather, MOOCs are open to the world and attract a variety of participants with different objectives: ambitious high school students, students in traditional classes using MOOCs as reference sources for coursework elsewhere, and curious citizens using MOOCs like a public library. It is not enough simply to find the difference between enrollments and completions. It will be far more interesting and strategically valuable to better understand who takes MOOCs, what their relationship is to traditional education systems, and what motivates them to register for and complete online education programs.

While demographic data about MOOC participation is still difficult to find, there are some sample profiles with numbers. Steve Kolowich provides a glimpse in "Early demographic data hints at what type of student takes a MOOC," in *Inside Higher Ed*. The article reviewed survey results from one Coursera MOOC.

Coursera began when co-founder Andrew Ng taught a course called Machine Learning to 104,000 online students. According to Kolowich, half of the 14,045 respondents to a demographic survey were full-time professionals employed in technology. Forty-one percent of those identified themselves as "professionals currently working in the software industry" and nine percent as professionals working in other areas of the information technology industry. Nearly twenty

Michael Nanfito

percent were graduate students in traditional post-secondary education programs and another 11.6 percent identified themselves as undergraduates. Of the remaining respondents, 3.5 percent were unemployed or employed outside of the technology industry; one percent were enrolled in a K-12 school program, and 11.5 percent identified themselves as "other." When a subset of 11,686 participants was asked why they chose to take the course, thirty-nine percent responded that they were "curious about the topic," another 30.5 percent said they were interested in the potential to "sharpen the skills" used in their current position and eighteen percent were interested in the course as a means to "position [themselves] for a better job."[7]

Kolowich also reviewed data on an electrical engineering course, Circuits and Electronics, offered by edX. Like the data from the Coursera sample, the numbers are by no means comprehensive, but they do provide a basic view into the demographics of the participants who completed the course. Of 155,000 who registered, 9,300 passed the midterm exam, 8,200 made it as far as the final exam, and just over 7,000 passed the final with the option to receive an informal certificate of completion from edX. Kolowich notes that the age distribution of participants who made it to the end lean towards what we in higher education would call "nontraditional" students (although Clay Shirkey would argue that the nontraditional is increasingly the norm). Half of the participants were twenty-six or older while about forty-five percent were traditional college-aged students. Five percent identified as current high school students. The oldest was seventy-four, the youngest fourteen. Roughly thirty percent said they did not have a bachelor's degree while thirty-seven percent said they did. Twenty-eight percent claimed to have a master's degree and six percent a doctorate.[8]

Yvonne Belanger, who leads assessment and program evaluation at the Center for Instructional Technology at Duke University, recently published a summary of enrollment in Duke's first Coursera MOOC, Bioelectricity: A Quantitative Approach. Only about three hundred fifty of the approximately 12,700 registrants took the final exam—a dropout rate of ninety-seven percent.

Noting that "Student motivation in the MOOC environment is a significant area of interest to stakeholders at Duke and elsewhere," Belanger surveyed the participants with both pre- and post-course questions about their reasons for enrolling and completing the course. As part of a Coursera-supplied, pre-course survey instrument, "fun and enjoyment" were identified as important reasons for enrolling by a large majority of students.

On her post-course survey, students responded to a broader range of questions in which Belanger separated motivations for enrolling from initial intentions once enrolled. Respondents had the option to select all applicable choices. Mining information in user-supplied comments from both the survey and course discussion forums, Belanger identified four categories of participant motivation including Lifelong learning, Social experience, Convenience, Exploration of online learning.[9]

Writing on the Center for Instructional Technology blog, Belanger notes that motivations for MOOC participants vary, and she cautions against comparing MOOC demographics and completion rates to traditional campus courses. She identifies five reasons that may help us understand why individuals sign up for MOOCs but fail to complete them:

1. A significant number (1/3 to 1/2) of those who registered for the course never actually started it. As Belanger says "Based on data about Duke's Coursera courses,

anywhere from 1/3 to 1/2 of students who enroll in our MOOCs never come back and log in after the course begins."

2. A majority of those who registered for the course never intended to finish it. According to the statistics gathered by Belanger, "earning the Statement of Accomplishment . . . was very important to only about 10% of them."

3. The course was open to anyone without restriction. Several factors and requirements contribute to limiting class sizes and participation in traditional courses including "a secondary school education, the admissions office, the bursar's office, whether or not they've passed the prerequisites as defined on our campus, and the number of seats in the classroom." These requirements are absent in MOOCs and this contributes to the inflated registration numbers.

4. For many, perhaps most, there is no concrete value in completing the course. Qualifying for a "Statement of Accomplishment" that currently carries little if any credibility beyond individual satisfaction fails to motivate most registrants.

5. The course simply was not a priority for most of those who registered. Despite curiosity and interest in the potential of the course, most have more pressing things to attend to: "In our largest course, about 2/3 say they work either full or part time, with full time outnumbering part time 2:1. About 1/3 are currently students (including pre-college, undergrad and grad). And quite a few are students who work."

(**Source**: Blogpost, "Participation And Completion Of Moocs," Yvonne Belanger, March 1, 2013. http://cit.duke.edu/blog/2013/03/participation-and-completion-of-moocs/)

It is important also to note that MOOCs have successfully connected participants from across the globe. EdX speaks to this strategic motive on its website: "Along with offering online courses, the institutions will use edX to research how students learn and *how technology can transform learning–both on-campus and worldwide*" [emphasis added]. So where are MOOC participants located? What are the factors that contribute to or challenge the global reach of MOOCs?

Participation data from the course "Internet History, Technology, and Security," taught by Charles Severance, Associate Professor in the School of Information at the University of Michigan, through Coursera provides some insight into global demographics. Severance conducted his own survey to determine the geographic distribution of participants. Severance describes his methodology, noting its limitations:

"This data is from a survey conducted of the students enrolled (4701 responses) in the Internet, History, Technology and Security course taught on Coursera on July-September 2012. The data was open-ended responses to the question, 'Where are you taking the course from (State / Country)?' The open-ended user responses were submitted to the Google Maps geocoding API and as such likely to be imperfect and/or approximate. There was no cleaning of the data either before or after submitting it to the Google geocoding API. All data including location label displayed when you hover over a marker comes from the geocoding API and its approximation of the location - no end-user entered data is present on this page."[10]

Though a rough estimate of a sampling of data from one course, the data illustrates general views into the demographics of MOOC participation at the global scale. There is heavy representation from North America, Europe, and South Asia, specifically India. There is slightly less participation from South America and East Asia.

Michael Nanfito

Participation from African nations and Central Asia is sparse. This correlates with more general data provided by Coursera on the geographic representation of participation in its MOOCs.

Kris Olds, in "On the territorial dimensions of MOOCs," notes the importance of using geospatial representations of MOOC usage and demographic data on access to Internet and telecommunications to understand regional and national capacity to participate in such courses. He believes forwarding a monolithic "notion of a singular 'global' or 'international' category" to MOOC participation is misguided. Internet access and telecommunications bandwidth is clearly increasing, but there are significant limitations even within wired countries.[11]

Olds also points out that the disciplinary content of MOOCs is worth reviewing when examining geospatial demographics. For example, many of the first MOOCs were on information technology, specifically computer science and software development—topics with a global reach. Other topics may be of more regional or local interest. When Tucker Balch, a professor in the School of Interactive Computing at Georgia Tech, taught Computational Investing, Part I, via Coursera in Fall 2012, the overwhelming proportion of those completing the MOOC were from the United States.[12] Balch surveyed participants and collected responses from 2,350 of his 53,205 students.

At this time, demographic data is inadequate. Effective decision-making by campuses will require much better metrics and data. The preliminary work of observers like Belanger, Hill, and Jordan is useful, however, and will influence the development of projects analyzing enrollment and completion rates.

Udacity and San Jose State University, for example, are

currently at work on a project demonstrating the potential of building data gathering directly into the delivery of MOOCs. In January 2013, they announced the joint creation and delivery of three introductory mathematics classes. For Udacity, a stated objective of the pilot is to investigate strategies to bolster retention by requiring participating SJSU students to have more "skin in the game" by paying $150 per credit (standard per-credit fees in the California state university system range from $450-$750). By framing these "MOOCs" in the context of commitment and reward, SJSU and Udacity hope to create a laboratory for defining metrics, establishing baselines, and measuring success. Such projects will help develop successful and scalable online programs with defined retention strategies. As more data on MOOCs is generated and compiled, campus leaders will have better decision-making tools regarding them.

Whether or not you are part of a large state university system or affiliated with an elite campus with whom providers like Coursera are willing to work, you need to develop an assessment plan to help you consider MOOCs as potential solutions to enrollment problems.

- Update enrollment needs at your institution.

- Determine your institutional ability to develop and deliver MOOCs.

- Decide if you will work with external MOOC providers.

- Consider working with an outside agency to develop a critical review of providers.

- Work with faculty to define courses that are

Michael Nanfito

candidates for online teaching.

- Define an inclusive approval process that involves your faculty.

- Define financial aid eligibility as it applies to MOOCs.

- Determine whether you will charge for course enrollments.

- Determine how you will manage MOOC data in your student information systems.

Chapter 3: Endnotes

4. Shirky, "Your Massively Open Offline College Is Broken."

5. Hill, "Emerging Student Patterns in MOOCs: A Graphical View."

6. Jordan, "Katy Jordan: Researching Education and Technology."

7. Kolowich, "Who Takes MOOCs?".

8. Ibid.

9. Belanger and Thornton, "Bioelectricity."

10. Severance, "Visualizing the Geographic Distribution of My Coursera Course."

11. Olds, "On the Territorial Dimensions of MOOCs."

12. Balch, "MOOC Student Demographics."

Michael Nanfito

Chapter 3: The Demographics of MOOCs - Recommended Readings

Allen, I. Elaine, and Jeff Seaman. "Ten Years of Tracking Online Education in the United States." Babson Survey Research Group, January 2013.

Balch, Tucker. "MOOC Student Demographics." *The Augmented Trader*, January 27, 2013.

Belanger, Yvonne. "Participation and Completion of MOOCs." *Center for Instructional Technology, Duke University*, March 1, 2013.

Belanger, Yvonne, and Jessica Thornton. "Bioelectricity: A Quantitative Approach Duke University's First MOOC" (2013).

Carey, Kevin. "California Shifts the Ground Under Higher Education." The Chronicle of Higher Education. *The Conversation*, March 13, 2013.

Edmundson, Mark. "Will MOOCs Open Elite Universities to Excessive Corporate Influence? (essay)." *Inside Higher Ed*, October 12, 2012.

Gardner, Lee, and Jeffrey R. Young. "California's Move Toward MOOCs Sends Shock Waves, but Key Questions Remain Unanswered." *The Chronicle of Higher Education*, March 14, 2013, sec. Government.

Hill, Phil. "Emerging Student Patterns in MOOCs: A Graphical View." *e-Literate*, March 6, 2013. http://mfeldstein.com/emerging_student_patterns_in_moocs_graphical_view/.

———. "The Most Thorough Summary (to Date) of MOOC Completion Rates." *e-Literate*, February 26, 2013. http://mfeldstein.com/the-most-thorough-summary-to-date-of-mooc-completion-rates/.

Jordan, Katy. "MOOC Completion Rates." Accessed March 18, 2013. http://www.katyjordan.com/MOOCproject.html.

Kolowich, Steve. "Early Demographic Data Hints at What Type of Student Takes a MOOC." *Inside Higher Ed*. Accessed March 6, 2013.

———. "SUNY Signals Major Push Toward MOOCs and Other New Educational Models." The Chronicle of Higher Education. *The Wired Campus*, March 20, 2013.

Leber, Jessica. "How MOOCs Could Meet the Challenge of Providing a Global Education." *MIT Technology Review*, March 15, 2013.

Olds, Kris. "On the Territorial Dimensions of MOOCs." *Inside Higher Ed*, December 3, 2012.

Regalado, Antonio. "Massive Open Online Courses in the Developing World." *MIT Technology Review*, November 12, 2012.

Rivard, Ry. "California Academic Leaders Oppose Outsourcing Plan." *Inside Higher Ed*, March 28, 2013.

———. "Florida and New York Look to Centralize and Expand Online Education." *Inside Higher Ed*, March 27, 2013.

Severance, Charles. "Visualizing the Geographic Distribution of My Coursera Course," September 30, 2012. http://www.dr-chuck.com/csev-blog/2012/09/geographic-distribution-of-my-coursera-course/.

Shirky, Clay. "How to Save College." *The Awl*, February 7, 2013.

"The Big Three MOOC Providers." *The New York Times*, November 2, 2012, sec. Education / Education Life.

Watters, Audrey. "Top Ed-Tech Trends of 2012: Data and Learning Analytics." *Inside Higher Ed*, December 20, 2012.

Young, Jeffrey R. "California State U. Will Experiment With Offering Credit for MOOCs." *The Chronicle of Higher Education*, January 15, 2013, sec. Technology.

Part 2: Nuts and Bolts

Chapter 4: Impacts of online learning technologies

Comparatively few of the nation's more than 4,000 degree-granting American colleges or universities . . . have the personnel, instructional and technological infrastructure . . . to invest in launching their own MOOCs.[13]

—Kenneth C. Green

Practically speaking, MOOCs are a platform of bundled technologies. If you sign with Coursera, Udacity, edX, or other xMOOC providers, you'll make use of the technology bundle that they provide. If you elect to develop your own cMOOC, you likely already provide support to your on-campus constituents for most of the technologies used to deliver such MOOCs—though you may not have consciously connected them in the same manner, or at the same scale. cMOOCs make use of information systems commonly found on campus: an LMS, wikis, blogs, social media, and video and videoconferencing tools.

But MOOCs are more than just the technology that drives them. MOOCs—especially cMOOCs—are personal learning networks, enabled by technology, that enable the learner to interact with and derive knowledge from other participants. Learners themselves take responsibility, create connections and develop networks of resources that contribute to their professional development and knowledge. In the context of these personal learning networks, the learner need not know other participants personally or ever meet in person.

These concepts underscore the thinking behind MOOCs and the rationale to aggregate the technologies brought together to create them. It is in this context that MOOCs have the potential to amplify the scope and scale of learning as well as your institutional influence and reach.

The potential of these technologies notwithstanding, there are issues your campus planning team should consider before finalizing a MOOC program. The nexus of existing technologies and the implementation of them at the scale of the MOOC amplify attendant (and pre-existing) issues—support and scalability, exposure and liability— that you will need to consider as you identify the extent to which you participate in the provision of MOOCs. The amplification of these issues will likely impact how your institution supports current practices should you decide to participate in and provide MOOCs.

In this chapter we'll briefly review the underlying technologies that enable MOOCs. We will outline the issues and challenges regarding user support, scalability, exposure, and liability that implementing technologies at the scale of the MOOC introduces. Throughout, we will include questions you will want to ask yourself regarding your institutional capacity to develop, support, and sustain MOOCs and online learning.

A brief review of the technologies that implement *and sustain* a MOOC

Learning Management System (LMS). Blackboard, Moodle, Sakai, and Instructure are examples of LMS services in place on campuses now. Common attributes of LMS services include: discussion forums, file exchange, text chat, whiteboard and screen sharing, student groups and portfolios, tests and test management, gradebooks, student participation tracking, and accessibility compliance. The LMS is more than likely the core of your current online learning effort. Significantly, the LMS is also generally at the core of many MOOC implementations, with attendant supporting technologies. It is important to note that deploying LMS for MOOCs will impact your current LMS programs.

Wikis. A wiki is essentially a website that allows users to add, modify, or delete content via a browser. Wikis are intentionally *participatory* and intended to be developed and used *collaboratively*, thus making them effective in the cMOOC environment. Wikis complement and may even replace centrally administered content management systems. The decentralized nature of wikis allows them to provide for efficient dissemination of information across an organization or community of practice. MediaWiki, DrupalWiki, and PBWorks are examples of wiki platforms in use on many college campuses.

Blogs. Wordpress, Drupal, Moveable Type, and Live Journal are popular blogs used in higher education. Ready-made templates make these blogs easy for users to implement quickly and to manage effectively. Academic bloggers have been making use of these resources for over a decade. Blogs are an effective tool, enabling reflection and participatory review from learners and instructors. As with wikis, the intentionally participatory nature of these resources makes them exceptionally relevant for MOOCs.

Videography. Lecture capture and videography are an important component of MOOCs. Short videos developed using simple desktop webcams and delivered via YouTube are easily accessible to participants. More ambitious producers use high-end videography talent and tools to develop broadcast-quality videos that employ multiple camera shots and sophisticated editing.

Social media and networking. Facebook, Twitter, LinkedIn, and Google+ are common social media sites used by faculty and students. MOOC participants have become acculturated to connecting via these resources and they use them quite effectively to stay connected, keep pace with trends, and share resources.

These technologies are in use today and have experienced widespread adoption by faculty, administrators, and students. However, programmatic support for them and for various other services varies, being dependent on available staff and budget. As you contemplate participation in MOOCs—whether as provider or participant—you need to consider the implications of such an expansive technology-enabled program in the context of your institutional mission, ability to provide support, and the potential for exposure and liability.

Consider this: MOOCs *amplify* pre-existing support challenges

Support for the MOOC: Does it scale? Are you prepared to support the communities of practice at the scale of MOOCs? For many colleges and universities, technology *support* is funded and staffed for current technology *implementation* with little room for exploration or innovation, especially where that exploration requires supporting users not formally affiliated with the institution.

Central IT provides fundamental (and approved) information technology resources to the campus. The policies are clear and the support model is documented. The constituents (registered students, faculty, and staff) work on campus. IT departments have a long history in the provision of these resources, know what to expect, have budgeted for system upgrades, license renewals, and incremental expansion, and are generally staffed to ensure appropriate response time to users troubleshooting issues and concerns.

Michael Nanfito

In addition to "fundamental" campus-supplied technology, however, faculty, staff, and students make use of remote wikis, blogs, and social media sites on their own, with no institutional support. The ubiquity and growth of these readily available online services has made it easy for users to adopt and incorporate them into research and study and to connect with colleagues and collaborators with little or no assistance from central IT. This reality of extra-institutional technology usage reveals a gap in programmatic provision and support of IT services. Campuses, it turns out, don't have a *comprehensive* account of technology usage by faculty and students in the pursuit of their research and scholarship. Faculty and staff routinely use external, discipline-specific technology resources developed and delivered by extramural professional associations to accomplish their work. Significantly, most would say that these technologies are also "fundamental" to their academic and professional success.

For example, the Modern Language Association (MLA) recently launched *MLA Commons*, a gathering space for humanists and others to work together, based on the Commons-in-a-Box resource developed by the City University of New York (CUNY). MLA Commons already had 1,361 active users as of March 2013. Users, primarily registered members of MLA, avail themselves of the Commons' networking resources without relying on the support of their host institution, since MLA provides both the resource and the support.

MLA Commons users fly under the local campus IT radar; their own institutions cannot know the extent of their activity with these tools, issues encountered, support received from providers, and what it would cost the campus to provide comparable services. From a strategic thinking perspective, this is an important point. There are (potentially) good and bad outcomes to effectively outsourcing academic technology resources and legitimizing faculty and staff usage of them.

On the other end of the spectrum, should your institution decide to implement MOOCs, you bring (remote) users onto the (local) IT support radar screen. You may be obligated to support their needs and troubleshoot their problems regardless of location and affiliation. The introduction of MOOCs, with their legions of outside users, into your existing services and support model will have an impact on the quality and timeliness of support for traditional, on-campus, constituents. With no experience at this scale, and no metric available, it may well prove difficult to quantify the extent of that impact.

Massive online technology failure: it *can* happen here. Even universities with great strength in technology and significant staff resources are challenged to support innovative technology implementation and usage on the scale of the MOOC. A recent event at the Georgia Institute of Technology is instructive.

In late January 2013, Georgia Tech offered the MOOC *Fundamentals of Online Education: Planning and Application*, taught by Fatimah Wirth, and hosted by Coursera. This course was intended to teach participants how to provide effective online learning with an emphasis on mastering the technologies involved in creating and delivering online courses and managing the issues engendered in this environment. The course description states clearly what would be learned: "This is an introductory course on the fundamentals of online education. You will learn how to convert your face-to-face class into a robust online course based on theory and

Michael Nanfito

practice."

The course description goes on to say, "In this course you will learn about the fundamentals of online education. The emphasis will be on planning and application. In the planning phase, you will explore online learning pedagogy, online course design, privacy and copyright issues, online assessments, managing an online class, web tools and Learning Management Systems. In the application phase, you will create online learning materials. The final project for the course will consist of you building an online course based on everything that you learned and created in the course."

More than 40,000 participants enrolled. Less than a week after the start, the course was shut down due to technical failure. As of March 2013, it was still unavailable.

Officials from Coursera and Georgia Tech confirmed that the technology facilitating small group discussion—Google Docs—had failed. Richard DeMillo, the director of Georgia Tech's Center for 21st Century Universities, said in a subsequent article in *Inside Higher Ed* ("Why the Online Ed MOOC Didn't Work") that support staff had not anticipated "any insurmountable problems" with the technology, going on to say that there "wasn't enough time for his staff to test the small group discussion features of Google Docs." Students who registered for the course responded with "a mixture of anger and humor to the implosion of the course, tweeting "Fundamentals of Online Education' MOOC, broke down in the first week. Cue scathing declarations of symbolism." DeMillo went on to stress the importance of experimentation: "If we tell people to just do safe things, we'll stifle innovation."[14] In the same article, Andrew Ng, co-founder of Coursera, said the decision to experiment with Google Docs for the small group discussion component of the course "didn't work well enough," despite being "really innovative." He provided assurances that Coursera will continue to develop quality control procedures that can be used before future course launches. He added that he was "proud we let instructors experiment with different formats."[15]

All of this is reasonable from the perspective of Coursera, a Silicon Valley startup experimenting with Higher Education technology ventures. Frankly, it is even understandable from the perspective of Georgia Tech, an institute with the stated mission to be "distinguished by its commitment to improving the human condition through advanced science and technology." These are the organizations and institutions that should be pushing the boundaries in just this manner. We rely on them to do just that. It is unclear, however, whether course participants *not* formally part of the in Georgia Tech community are as committed to being a part of the experiment in real time.

To be fair, while the 40,000-plus registration numbers are impressive and have shock value, we know that the number of MOOC *registrants* is orders of magnitude greater than the number who actually *complete* these courses. Nevertheless, even with the most ruthless calculation, based on statistics we have for MOOC course completion, over one thousand participants would likely have seen the course through to completion, had there been no technology failure. One thousand students is a big cohort of learners in a single course and the fact remains that the course was cancelled as a result of admittedly incomplete planning and testing by both vendor and institution. While there is value in experimentation, most students would probably prefer that it not occur on their time.

Massive exposure and liability: Are you legal? The

Michael Nanfito

Americans with Disabilities Act of 1990 (ADA) * Sec. 12132, Discrimination, states "... *no qualified individual with a disability shall, by reason of such disability, be excluded from participation in or be denied the benefits of services, programs, or activities of a public entity.*"[16] MOOC technologies greatly amplify existing issues regarding exposure and liability. As with scalability and support, challenges with respect to *accessibility, copyright,* and *fair use* will be magnified in a massive learning environment. You and your faculty and staff will need to consider institutional exposure as you contemplate entering the MOOC fray.

Academic libraries have long dealt with all of these issues regarding curricular materials. In October 2012, Brandon Butler of the Association of Research Libraries (ARL), in a brief on the legal and policy Issues that MOOC technology raises, wrote: "Some of the key legal issues that MOOCs raise for research libraries revolve around copyright and the use of copyrighted content in this new context, while others relate to open access and accessibility."[17]

Accessibility. Butler reminds us that the law "requires educational institutions to provide access to educational opportunities to all students on an equal basis without regard to disability." The Rehabilitation Act, passed in 1973, requires that any educational institution receiving federal funds must comply with regulations preventing discrimination of students with disabilities. Institutions must accommodate the needs of these students in order to ensure that they have equal opportunity to engage in their academic work: "The Americans with Disabilities Act (ADA) bars public colleges and universities from denying services, programs, or activities to disabled students, and prohibits private institutions from discriminating against disabled students, as well "[18]

Butler goes on to say that these requirements "apply to university efforts on MOOC platforms, despite their being cutting edge or pilot programs." He reminds us that the US Departments of Justice and Education have already "pursued this issue with respect to early efforts to adopt e-readers in universities, warning institutions that use of non-accessible Kindles, even for pilot programs, would violate both Section 504 and the ADA."[19]

[See US Dept. Justice, Joint "Dear Colleague" Letter: Electronic Book Readers, June 29, 2010, http://www2. ed.gov/about/offices/list/ocr/letters/colleague-20100629. html; US Dept. of Education, Office of Civil Rights, Frequently Asked Questions About the June 29, 2010, Dear Colleague Letter, May 26, 2011, http://www2.ed.gov/about/ offices/list/ocr/docs/dcl-ebook-faq-201105.pdf.]

Ensuring accessibility compliance is not easy. The design of commonly used technology (web pages, blogs, wikis, and PDFs) and their integration with assistive technology devices for use by individuals with disabilities is a significant concern and should be addressed at the front-end of course development and delivery rather than after the fact. It is more difficult and costly to re-engineer materials for accessibility to the disabled than to practice appropriate design from the outset. Academic libraries routinely take steps to make accessibility a priority, and, as Butler's brief illustrates, that ethos will by necessity extend to MOOC content.

Schools that actually have the available resources are generally able to cope with the challenge of ensuring accessibility of their online resources. For example, the Illinois Center for Information Technology and Web

Michael Nanfito

Accessibility at the University of Illinois at Urbana-Champaign has done a great deal of work developing criteria for evaluating instructional resources for ADA compliance. On their website they note specific challenges for colleges that decide to deploy online learning resources:

"If not designed with accessibility in mind, Learning Management Systems (LMS) can pose accessibility problems for students and instructors with disabilities . . . Some LMS tools—Discussions, Quizzes, Chat, or Wiki tools, for instance—can be more problematic than others. Learning Management Systems are becoming richer and more complex applications, and if they are not designed with accessibility in mind, it can be next to impossible to make them accessible and usable to users with various needs."[20]

Similarly, MIT works hard to ensure that the OpenCourseWare accessibility standards are met: "We spend a lot of time on the accessibility of PDFs . . . We work closely with the MIT Adaptive Technology for Information and Computing Lab to ensure that the MIT OpenCourseWare course sites are as accessible as possible."[21] (http://ocw.mit.edu/help/faq-technology/)

Schools like MIT, Georgia Tech, and the University of Illinois at Urbana-Champaign have significant resources to bring to bear on the development of accessibility-compliant resources. As your campus considers online learning in the context of institutional mission and strategic priorities, engage the campus and survey existing policies and practices including copyright, intellectual property (who owns MOOC content developed and delivered by your faculty?), and accessibility.

Fair Use and Copyright. In addition to accessibility,

MOOCs raise legal questions with respect to copyright and fair use. In February 2013, Stanford University Libraries hosted a panel on "MOOCs, Online Education, and the Library." One of the panelists, Merrilee Proffit, Senior Program Officer at OCLC Research, shared results from her research on Libraries and MOOCs. She pointed out "copyright issues are making universities cautious, since the classes most often provide access to learning materials to users outside the usual licensing institutions."[22]

Colleges and universities do well to maintain a cautious approach. It is not clear if MOOCs, especially when delivered in concert with for-profit providers, can assume legitimate use of course materials based on traditional applications of statutory exceptions or reliance on license agreements.

As for-profit providers and colleges and universities struggle to define business models for MOOCs, including potential revenue generation schemes, the status of a MOOC course as "non-profit" grows less certain. The more a MOOC partnership resembles for-profit publishing rather than non-profit teaching, the less likely it is that traditional teaching exceptions for colleges and libraries will apply to MOOCs. These traditional exceptions and licenses may require reexamination in the MOOC world.

Colleges and universities clearly have a part to play in helping to determine the next steps with respect to compliance and legitimate use in the context of MOOCs and online learning. Academic libraries in particular have a persistent role to play in identifying the issues and questions, then working with their institution, partner organizations, publishers and providers to define potential paths to success. The library investment in developing and managing relationships with publishers represents a

Michael Nanfito

significant resource in your consideration of MOOCs.

With respect to the modification of license agreements, Academic Impressions interviewed Kevin Smith, director of scholarly communications for Duke University's Perkins Library, in January 2013 ("How will MOOCs Affect Fair Use and Copyright Compliance?"). In the interview, Smith argues that colleges and university libraries "have a huge opportunity to establish new partnerships with copyright holders (publishers and various clearinghouses), developing agreements to use their materials in the MOOCs, because of the significant opportunity for the MOOC to raise the visibility of their materials."[23] Despite concerns to the contrary, Smith maintains that publishers will in fact be amenable to flexibility with respect to MOOCs specifically because of the expansive market that MOOC participants represent. Smith argues that instructors recommending (or requiring) texts will lead to spikes in sales for publishers. He describes a situation in which a publisher initially denied a request from an instructor to use copyrighted materials in a MOOC that she successfully used in her traditional classroom. Smith describes how his office persisted, asking the publisher's permissions office to check in with the marketing group: "Please talk with your marketing office. Because what is going to happen here is that 40,000-50,000 people are going to self-identify as interested in the topic, and your textbook will be recommended to them by a well-regarded authority. We have seen a number of instances in which a professor recommends a book and then sales spike because of the MOOC. So we have empirical evidence. It's marketing gold for a publisher."[24]

Not everyone shares Smith's enthusiasm, nor does every campus has the negotiating clout of larger academic libraries. However, as more schools develop and deliver mission-driven online learning programs, there is opportunity to identify new consortial approaches to leverage the "marketing power" of like-minded institutions. Campuses are poised to leverage the success of existing library consortial models to address the exposure and liability concerns that MOOCs and other online learning models raise. Institutions will do well to review their strategy for inter-institutional collaboration and cooperation, so as to position themselves successfully in negotiations with providers and publishers in the context and scope of expansive online learning models.

In addition to the significant concerns of support, exposure, and liability that implementation of MOOC-scale information technologies bring, there are other, technology-related issues to consider.

Bandwidth divide. Even if your campus is capable of *delivering* on the scale of the MOOC, you are part of an online ecosystem that is not created equal. There are very real obstacles to delivering online resources to users in the "last mile" of the network who are unable to *receive* your course because their network bandwidth is effectively nil.

As Jeffrey Young says in "'Bandwidth Divide' Could Bar Some People From Online Learning" (*Chronicle of Higher Education*, March 4, 2013), there is a chasm between the bandwidth haves and have-nots. "As more colleges rush to offer free online courses in the name of providing educational access to all, it's worth asking who might be left out for lack of high-speed Internet access to watch video lectures."[25] Young goes on to cite Martin Hilbert, researcher at the University of Southern California's Annenberg School for Communication and Journalism, who argues that the bandwidth divide is real and is widening. Hilbert notes that the divide between those with high-speed Internet access and those with dial-up or cellphone access is "bigger than people think." Only 66 percent of American adults have broadband access at home, according to a May 2012 survey conducted by the Pew Internet & American Life Project. This has implications for the successful deployment of MOOCs by colleges regardless of the institution's capacity to develop, deliver, and support online learning. By design, the success of MOOCs and online learning depends in large part on the motivation and capacity of the learner. This must include the capacity to consume high bandwidth resources.

MOOCs are more than the technology that makes them work. MOOCs represent great potential for educational outreach and institutional influence. The development and deployment of MOOCs also represent significant challenges in ensuring effective user support and conscientious oversight with respect to commitment to access and intellectual property.

Online learning is not going away. It has become part of the academic ecosystem. In light of this, as you consider offering MOOCs as a part of your institutional mission and strategic planning, you need to ask yourself: What is your responsibility to participants in your institution's programming at this scale? How will you mesh strategy, innovation, and mission?

Planning Questions

1. Does your existing accessibility program scale to the audience of the MOOC?
2. Do your campus policies regarding copyright and fair use scale to the MOOC?
3. What is your institutional responsibility to ensure equal access to online resources, even when you offer

and provide them to users not necessarily affiliated with the campus?

4. How will existing library materials be used and incorporated into MOOC courses?
5. Does Fair Use apply?
6. Do your existing license agreements provide for MOOC usage?
7. Will publishers be amenable to modifying license agreements?
8. Is your academic library currently part of a local or regional consortium?
9. What leverage does that consortium provide with respect to publishers and licenses in the MOOC environment?

Chapter 4 Endnotes

13. Green, "Mission, MOOCs, & Money."

14. Jaschik, "Why the Online Ed MOOC Didn't Work."

15. Ibid.

16. "Americans with Disabilities Act of 1990, AS AMENDED with ADA Amendments Act of 2008."

17. Butler, "Issue Brief: Massive Open Online Courses: Legal and Policy Issues for Research Libraries."

18. Ibid.

19. Ibid.

20. Illinois Center for Information Technology and Web Accessibility, "A Comparison of Learning Management System Accessibility."

21. MIT OpenCourseware, "FAQ: Technology Free Online Course Materials."

22. Makokha, "In Case You Missed It: 'MOOCs, Online Education, and the Library' Report."

23. McDonald and Smith, "How Will MOOCs Affect Fair Use and Copyright Compliance?".

24. Ibid.

25. Young, "'Bandwidth Divide' Could Bar Some People From Online Learning."

Michael Nanfito

Chapter 4: Impacts of online learning technologies - Recommended Readings

"Americans with Disabilities Act of 1990, AS AMENDED with ADA Amendments Act of 2008." http://www.ada.gov/pubs/adastatute08.htm.

Butler, Brandon. "ARL Policy Notes, ARL Issue Brief: MOOCs + Libraries = ???" *ARL Policy Notes.*

———. "Issue Brief: Massive Open Online Courses: Legal and Policy Issues for Research Libraries."

"FAQ: Technology Free Online Course Materials." *MIT OpenCourseware*, n.d. http://ocw.mit.edu/help/faq-technology/.

Green, Kenneth C. "Mission, MOOCs, & Money." *Association of Governing Boards*, February 2013.

Howard, Jennifer. "For Libraries, MOOCs Bring Uncertainty and Opportunity." The Chronicle of Higher Education. *The Wired Campus*, March 25, 2013.

Illinois Center for Information Technology and Web Accessibility. "A Comparison of Learning Management System Accessibility." http://presentations.cita.illinois.edu/2011-03-csun-lms/.

Kolowich, Steve. "Georgia Tech and Coursera Try to Recover From MOOC Stumble." The Chronicle of Higher Education. *The Wired Campus*, February 4, 2013.

Makokha, Joseph Maloba. "In Case You Missed It: 'MOOCs, Online Education, and the Library' Report." *Stanford University Libraries*, February 27, 2013.

McDonald, Steven, and Kevin Smith. "How Will MOOCs Affect Fair Use and Copyright Compliance?" *Academic Impressions*, January 11, 2013.

Morrison, Debbie. "How NOT to Design a MOOC: The Disaster at Coursera and How to Fix It." *Online Learning Insights A Blog About Open and Online Education*, February 1, 2013.

Perez, Thomas E., and Russlynn Ali. "Joint 'Dear Colleague' Letter: Electronic Book Readers," June 29, 2010. http://www2.ed.gov/about/offices/list/ocr/letters/colleague-20100629.html.

Rivard, Ry. "MOOCs Prompt Some Faculty Members to Refresh Teaching Styles." *Inside Higher Ed*, March 5, 2013.

"Why the Online Ed MOOC Didn't Work." *Inside Higher Ed*, February 5, 2013.

Young, Jeffrey R. "'Bandwidth Divide' Could Bar Some People From Online Learning." *The Chronicle of Higher Education*, March 4, 2013, sec. Technology.

Michael Nanfito

Chapter 5: Can MOOCs be made to add up?

While strong majorities of presidents agree that going online should be good for both enrollments and revenue, there is less evidence about just how much new net revenue online education actually produces—if any.[26] —Kenneth C. Green

A Moody's report released on January 16, 2013, gave the entire higher education sector a negative outlook. The report identified a downward shift even for elite institutions with existing demand and significant brand recognition. "The U.S. higher education sector had hit a critical juncture in the evolution of its business model," wrote Eva Bogarty, the report's author. "Most universities will have to lower their cost structures to achieve long-term financial sustainability and to fund future initiatives."[27] The report suggests several strategies for institutions to use MOOCs to advantage, including granting credit for a fee, licensing courses, and increasing efficiency by expanding the number of students an individual faculty member can serve.

The report further ratcheted up enthusiasm for the implementation of MOOCs. As a result corporate and institutional *investments* and *expectations* for MOOCs are higher than ever. It is anticipated that *enrollments*, *revenue*, and *profitability* will increase with the development and deployment of MOOCs. But will the numbers add up? Are the proposed business models and monetization schemes sustainable?

Setting the Stage: massive investment and hedged bets. Think of higher education as a boomtown along the lines of Seattle during the dot.com boom of the 1990s. Venture capitalists, state universities, private colleges, and for-profit schools are all looking for investment opportunities and calculating how much money to gamble. Higher-education investment in this space can take many forms: capital, infrastructure, faculty, and staff are areas ripe for responsible investment linked to *mission* and *strategy* (rather, it is to be hoped, than investment driven by insecurity and apprehension). Venture capital has been investing in corporate startups and technology platforms; academic institutions will invest in partnerships, faculty, staff, and programs.

Determined to benefit from a market they see as ripe for Clayton Christensen-style "disruption," venture capitalists have been pouring millions into education technology start-ups. Investments in such companies tripled in the last decade, rising from $146 million in 2002 to $429 million in 2011, according to the National Venture Capital Association.[28]

This isn't the first time colleges and universities have grown panicky over technological disruption. A similar wave hit higher education in the 1990s. As Kenneth C. (Casey) Green reflects, during the dot.com frenzy, the expectation on campus held that being "online" offered great potential with minimal investment. Posting syllabi and web pages for students accustomed to sitting in front of screens would give educational institutions unprecedented reach through "eyeballs and click-through," in the terminology of those hype-heavy days. College administrators and trustees grew fearful that by failing to go online, they would cede the advantage to early-adopting institutions.[29]

As Green points out, neither the market potential nor the disruptions materialized. The threatened disruptions and the predicted disadvantages tended to fade away,

Michael Nanfito

balance and harmony was restored, and everyone landed pretty much where they started, persistently reviewing and implementing academic technologies at a comfortable pace and making slow, steady progress.

The dot.com era also taught some enduring lessons to higher-education administrators. New positions in instructional technology were created; "blended librarians," with a mix of traditional librarianship and newfound facility with digital technologies, emerged. Academic Technology groups formed under IT or the Library or in the Learning Center. Campuses investigated and implemented such pragmatic technologies as learning management systems and digital asset management services. Institutions modified or developed policies to deal with copyright, intellectual property, and privacy in an online world. Many institutions began to share lectures, courses, and even sporting events via the web. Faculty, staff, and students explored and adopted blogs and social media. Academic institutions and supporting organizations now routinely broadcast online seminars via high-definition videoconferencing.

The academy, in other words, took on the surge of web-based technology and learned some hard-won lessons, the knowledge from which now resides in your faculty and staff. That knowledge is capital you can reinvest in a strategy for managing the current wave of enthusiasm for MOOCs. As for-profit firms increase their investment in online learning technologies, you must take a similar accounting of the resources available to you, and plan how to re-deploy them in the exploration and implementation of MOOCs.

When the dot.com wave crested at the turn of the millennium, money and corporate enthusiasm for the higher education sector disappeared. But today's investors are convinced that conditions are different this time around. Advances in technology on campus, a (misguided) belief in near-universal wireless access and high-speed internet connections, and an increasing confidence in cloud-based systems are providing entrepreneurs access to money and resources previously reserved for other markets. These resources are coming from venture capitalists and foundations alike.

The Bill & Melinda Gates Foundation, for example, has long been active in funding education, and its investments are growing: In 2012, the Foundation invested $2 million in the social network/student engagement startup Inigral. In November 2012, Gates contributed $895,453 to help the American Council on Education (ACE) establish a *Presidential Innovation Lab*, where college leaders can discuss MOOCs and other new business models for higher education. The Gates Foundation contribution is part of larger $3 million package of MOOC-related grants.

In the keynote address at the 2013 *South by Southwest Edu* conference, Bill Gates argued that more venture capitalists and corporations must invest in developing education technology and services to "kick-start new ways of teaching with technology." He shared a chart showing that education accounts for only one percent of all venture-capital investment. Acknowledging that education has never been an active R&D sector, he noted that "we're going to have to grow this" by "developing a gold standard of proving that something works," and identifying and improving how schools and colleges can share learning analytics data.[30]

Online learning is well established by now, and will continue to grow. How will you prepare and invest responsibly at your institution? What metrics must you identify and what dashboards must you develop to ensure that your institution will provide high-quality, reliable, credentialed online coursework for the next generation of learners?

These questions are worth posing and answering as aggressive investors of millions in technology products and services close in on your campus with intentions to sell you their solutions. How will you organize to invest in and implement effective, contemporary, on-line learning strategies?

Partner with Providers or Go It Alone? As you consider and investigate your online learning options, it will become clear that you may not be allowed to partner with the current major MOOC providers, who traffic on their exclusivity. If you decide to provide MOOCs, you will develop and deliver them on your own or in collaboration with other campuses also excluded from such partnerships. This will affect the nature and breadth of your investment strategy.

At the time of this writing, a tiny fraction of the four thousand-plus colleges and universities in the United States are included in such MOOC delivery services as Coursera and edX. Currently, Coursera is contractually required to limit campus partnerships to the sixty-two elite institutions that are members of the Association of American Universities. Coursera's contract with the University of California, Santa Cruz, spells it out: "It is Company's intent to offer on its Platform only Content provided by top-quality educational institutions. Within North America, Company will host and provide only Content provided by universities that are a member of the Association of American Universities." This is consistent with the Coursera vision and mission statement: "We are a social entrepreneurship company that partners with the top universities in the world to offer courses online for anyone to take, for free. We envision a future where the top universities are educating not only thousands of students, but millions. Our technology enables the best professors to teach tens or hundreds of thousands of students."[31] EdX, openly exclusive from the beginning, includes even fewer partnering institutions. If your institution is not on these elite lists and you are determined to develop and deliver MOOCs, you need to develop an investment plan of your own.

Invest in Faculty and Staff. Elite institutions and corporations flush with cash are investing huge sums in software, platforms, systems, and services to further online learning, which is unquestionably here to stay. Is your institution adequately prepared to develop and deliver online courses in this environment? Adjust your investment strategy with this in mind, and synch it with your institutional mission.

From Project to Program. Diana Oblinger and Brian Hawkins of Educause drafted an exemplary review of the fundamentals of successful online learning programming in 2006. Entitled "The Myth about Online Course Development," it is worthy of review and should be shared with all campus stakeholders involved in development of your overall strategic planning process. They identify four fundamental questions you should ask:

1. What is the best use of your faculty?

2. Do you have a process for strategically investing in online course development?

3. Do you confuse providing content with creating and delivering learning environments?

4. What is the desired return on investment in online course development and delivery?

The "traditional" method of investing in the development of online learning has relied heavily on providing release time and stipends to individual faculty with a modicum of technical expertise. These courses generally re-created the classroom lecture on the web. Oblinger and Hawkins argue that this model must be jettisoned in favor of a team approach to the development of online learning resources:

Developing and delivering effective online courses requires pedagogy and technology expertise possessed by few faculty. Good pedagogy implies that the instructor can develop targeted learning objectives. Online instruction is more than a series of readings posted to a Web site; it requires deliberate instructional design that hinges on linking learning objectives to specific learning activities and measurable outcomes. Few faculty have had formal education or training in instructional design or learning theory. To expect them to master the instructional design needed to put a well-designed course online is unrealistic. A more effective model is to pair a faculty member with an instructional designer so that each brings unique skills to the course-creation process.

This call to invest in faculty and staff development is echoed by Dr. Charlie McCormick, Provost at Schreiner University, who has been responsible for developing that institution's successful online learning program. When asked what he would do differently were he to embark on this effort now, he advised moving from the individual faculty approach to an institutional program model: "Provide more faculty development earlier in the process. Shift from the familiar individual faculty development (based on release time and stipend for individual course development) to institution-wide programmatic development. Develop a deliberate, well-articulated program with enough partnership and inclusion to enable faculty to see where their work fits into the larger institutional structure."

This model represents a significant shift in funding, planning, and organizational development for most campuses and will require close partnership and consultation with faculty, staff, and students. In the frenzy to offer MOOCs, faculty and other stakeholders are not always involved in the decision-making process or the negotiations. This is an opportunity to engage in an inclusive planning process to ensure institution-wide engagement.

Kenneth E. Hartman, a senior fellow at Edventures and the former president of Drexel eLearning at Drexel University, has specific recommendations for institutions in the process of developing their online learning programs. Hartman says that once you have taken account of your resources and articulated your strategy, you must "communicate the 'why' to key stakeholders from the top to the bottom of the organization, including board members, faculty, deans, students and alumni." You should incentivize faculty and staff and integrate them, at the institutional level described by McCormick, into your program. Develop the means to compensate these colleagues by distributing revenue from online courses to such support-related scholarly work as professional conferences, new equipment and resources, and internships.[32]

In order to make the investment, enrollment, revenue,

and overhead numbers add up, you will need to develop an inclusive, engaging, and deliberate program that is not about *MOOCs* alone but about the mission of the campus, the nature of learning with twenty-first century tools, and your strategy to succeed. The flurry of investments elsewhere has given rise to increased expectations everywhere. We need to identify the return on those investments, the viability of revenue projections, and sustainable business models in support of both.

Add it up: revenue dreams and abstract business models. MOOCs might be described as rough-hewn revenue sources in search of a business model. Globalization; democratization; and revenue generation through increased enrollments, certification and matchmaking between employers and MOOC participants are all posited as reasons to climb aboard the MOOC bandwagon.

Much is made of the potential locked inside the scope and scale of MOOCs, and expectations ride high on the notion that advertised enrollment numbers will translate into increased revenue. References to Google and other titans of the Internet eyeballs-on-the-page metrics are common, noting that Google's business model of ad-supported search was developed and implemented long after launch and site traffic increased. The projected revenue streams for MOOCS is similarly tied to "traffic volume" and is only vaguely articulated in the contracts between for-profit MOOC providers and their client colleges and universities.

But MOOCs are neither free nor easy. They take time and resources to develop and deploy. The overhead notwithstanding, for-profit firms and colleges and universities are plunging ahead, confident that the investment will be worth the ambiguous returns. But do the numbers add up?

Despite vague gestures towards potential revenue, usually cautious higher ed institutions have leapt into deals with vendors like Coursera. The contract between Coursera and the University of Michigan, obtained and published under a Freedom of Information Act request, reveals that no one, not even Coursera, knows exactly how MOOCs will generate revenue. A brief section of the agreement, entitled "Possible Company Monetization Strategies," lists eight potential revenue streams that are short on detail. Briefly:

1. Certification. Coursera provides non-credit-bearing, university-branded certificates available for purchase by participants.

2. Secure assessments. Coursera may provide identity verification to students (end-users) for a fee.

3. Employee recruiting. With student consent, Coursera provides access to student data to prospective employers. Student contact information remains confidential.

4. Employee or University screening. Coursera will provide prospective employers and/or universities access to prospective employees or students to assess level of expertise.

5. Human-provided tutoring or manual grading. Coursera will provide access to paid tutors and graders.

6. Corporate/University enterprise model. Coursera will provide access to an "enterprise" version of the course for employee training.

7. Sponsorships. With the approval of the university and the instructor, Coursera will permit third-party sponsorship of MOOC courses by foundations and/or corporations.

8. Tuition fees. Following mutual agreement by the

university and Coursera, a tuition fee may be charged for access to "certain courses."

Per the contract, the universities will get six to fifteen percent of revenue, depending on the duration of the course. Institutions will also get twenty percent of profits after costs and previous revenue are paid.

Any significant revenue derived from these models is necessarily structured around the massive enrollment data discussed earlier. As Jeffrey Young of the *Chronicle of Higher Education* reports, Daphne Koller, co-founder of Coursera, describes the rationale very clearly: "What we're doing is one instructor, 50,000 students. This is the way to bend the cost curves." Koller goes on to say, "Our VC's keep telling us that if you build a Web site that is changing the lives of millions of people, then the money will follow."[33]

Coursera is following a typical Silicon Valley start-up model: Build fast and demonstrate a user install base and hope the money will follow. Appreciation for that model is echoed by some in higher education: "Part of what Coursera's gotten right is that it makes more sense to build your user base first and then figure out later how to monetize it, than to worry too much at the beginning about how to monetize it," said Edward Rock, University of Pennsylvania Provost and director of their open course initiatives. (The University of Pennsylvania has developed sixteen Coursera courses, each costing approximately $50,000 to create. Videography and course support staff represent the most significant expenses.)[34]

Venture capitalists do not invest out of charity. Their objective is profit. But even edX, a not-for-profit MOOC collaboration between Harvard and MIT, needs to generate revenue, if not profit. In that context, edX has two models for university partnerships: the *university self-service model* and the *edX-supported model.*

The university self-service model allows a participating university to freely use edX's platform as a learning-management system for courses as long as edX receives part of any revenue generated by the course. EdX does not contribute to the development of the course. EdX collects the first $50,000 generated by the course, or $10,000 from each recurring course. The organization and the university partner each receive fifty percent of all revenue beyond that threshold.

In the edX-supported model, edX provides production assistance to universities for their MOOCs. EdX will charge $250,000 for each new course, plus $50,000 for each time a course is offered for an additional term. Although this model requires payment up front, potential returns to the university are high *if a course ends up making money.* Just as in the self-service model, edX will receive the first $50,000 for a new course, $10,000 for a recurring one. Beyond that, the university receives seventy percent of any additional revenue. Although the edX models provide more generous revenue sharing to universities than Coursera does, the income realized by the university comes only after edX has collected its cut.

The challenge is making money in the first place. EdX is as fuzzy as Coursera on how revenue will be generated.

Potential Monetization Models. Most MOOC vendors have responded to questions about their financial model by identifying various revenue streams. As you work to connect your institutional strategy and mission to the potential of MOOCs, you need to be aware of the monetization models that commercial vendors are developing. Understanding the nature and scope of their potential will help you make decisions about where your institution fits in the MOOC community.

Proctored exams and certification. The American Council on Education (ACE) is participating with Coursera and Udacity, using subject experts to assess five Coursera courses and four Udacity courses to determine if they merit transfer credits. Once the courses are deemed worthy, students who complete them can take identity-verified proctored exams for a fee and get an ACE Credit transcript (a certification that two thousand universities already accept for credit).

Coursera is developing partnerships with online proctoring companies to use Webcams and "keystroke biometrics" software to analyze patterns and rhythms of typing as a sort of keyboarding fingerprint. Coursera's remote-proctoring strategy has encouraged other MOOC providers, including edX and Udacity, to adopt competing strategies. Unlike Coursera's online proctoring, these organizations will use the four hundred fifty testing centers run by Pearson to allow students to take final exams in person and receive a certificate of completion. Udacity will charge $89.00, and edX anticipates fees for their exams will be under $100.00.

In this model, if fifty thousand people start a course, five thousand finish, and five hundred to one thousand are motivated to pay an assumed fee of $90.00 for a certificate of completion, the MOOC vendor would realize gross revenues of between $45,000 and $90,000. The university's share of that will be significantly smaller, of course, depending upon its contract with the vendor.

To help with students' "motivation" to complete the course and pay for the certificate, Coursera has developed a service called "Signature Track." This consists of designating specific courses as Signature Track courses and charging for the certificate up front: "If you're excited to participate or want to learn more, simply enroll in one of the above courses and you will be notified when you can join. The price for joining a course's Signature Track will be between $30-$100 per course." Signature Track could front-load revenue streams and facilitate more "skin in the game" for students, which could in turn increase course retention.

As you calculate the revenue from MOOC monetization models under vendor contracts, recall that your take is going to be considerably smaller.

Matchmaking. Bypassing exams, credits, and credentialing altogether, MOOC vendors may serve as "headhunters" for companies interested in their/your students.

Udacity has launched a job portal with plans to match students with companies that have signed with Udacity for this service. Some three hundred fifty companies have signed up, and Udacity has placed about twenty students. Coursera also notified students that they could participate in job-placement services in which Coursera uses analytics to scan student data, identifies matches between students and employers, and—with student permission—introduces the two to one another.

Assuming MOOC enrollments of fifty thousand, the general thinking is that even a relatively small proportion of successful matchmaking efforts will generate significant revenue to both the vendor and its partner institution. Working from the model in which typical headhunters receive fees equivalent to twenty percent of a candidate's starting salary, the vendors are betting on income of around $10,000 – $15,000 per match.

Michael Nanfito

Putting Potential into Practice: small sample of programs Antioch University and Coursera. In fall 2012, Coursera entered into a contract with Antioch University, allowing Antioch to license MOOCs developed by Coursera's university partners. Antioch will offer these MOOCs for credit as part of a bachelor's degree program.

The deal will help Coursera and its partner institutions develop a revenue stream from licensing MOOCs. This could potentially develop into a product that Coursera could sell to colleges: a packaged platform with instructors, course content, tools for student engagement, and assessment. The model may be a natural extension of the familiar learning management system (LMS). Coursera and its university partners will receive an undisclosed amount from Antioch for permission to use these courses, which include courses from Duke University and the University of Pennsylvania. Coursera's university partners retain intellectual property rights to their courses.

The potential for revenue sharing suggests the following scenario, with its interesting opportunities for faculty as well as institutions:

- Universities work with Coursera to develop MOOCs to be offered through Coursera.

- Schools decide to license some courses for a fee.

- Coursera shares the gross revenue and net profit with the universities.

- Faculty who developed the course also receive revenue.

Although there is potential revenue sharing here, it is limited to campuses contractually able to partner with

Coursera. Until other vendors create similar models and until Coursera's contract removes the restriction to work only with members of the American Association of Universities (AAU), most institutions will not be able to take advantage of this revenue stream.

San Jose State University and Udacity. State universities and community colleges in California are under the gun. Overcrowding, access to classes, and crushing student debt are forcing state and higher education leaders to find innovative solutions. Some of the more controversial proposals include MOOCs. As mentioned earlier, San Jose State University and Udacity announced a project to jointly create and deliver three introductory mathematics classes. The courses will be available to San Jose State students for credit at a cost of $150.00—again, not free, but less than the $450.00-$750.00 students would usually pay.

In addition to the potential of developing solid metrics to measure and improve retention in online courses, the project may be a model of revenue sharing. If it continues past its pilot phase, SJSU retains fifty-one percent of any revenue after costs are recovered, and Udacity gets forty-nine percent. The project also may provide a model for faculty receipt of compensation for contributing to the development of MOOCs. Faculty at San Jose State will be paid $15,000 to develop the pilot courses and will retain the intellectual-property rights to their materials.

Semester Online and 2U. Semester Online is a consortium of elite colleges and universities that includes Duke University, Emory University, Northwestern University and Washington University in St. Louis. According to the website, it is the first program to provide "the opportunity to take rigorous, online courses for credit from . . . leading universities" to undergraduates not actually enrolled at the institutions offering them. Semester Online is working with 2U (formerly known as 2tor) to provide a platform bringing elite schools online to "deliver rigorous, selective graduate degree and for-credit programs online." Semester Online began accepting applications in early 2013, with classes beginning that fall.

Other participating institutions include Brandeis University, Northwestern University, the Universities of North Carolina at Chapel Hill, Notre Dame, and Rochester, Vanderbilt University, and Wake Forest University.

Semester Online represents an iterative trend away from the "traditional" MOOC. The courses offered by the consortium will not be massive, free or open. Class sizes will be only fifteen to twenty students, who will earn college credit. Students will go through a selective admissions process established by the school offering the course, and they will have to pay. The originating institution will set course prices, which may equate to market rate. Duke University, for example, estimates that the cost will probably be about the same as an on-campus course—about $5,500, although details are still forthcoming.

Semester Online courses, by design, will not achieve the scale of MOOCs. And while the courses have the potential for the originating institutions to expand enrollments without buying property for new buildings, campus leaders are not hopeful that the program will significantly increase revenue or reduce tuition costs. As Steve Kolowich reported in the *Chronicle of Higher Education*, "campus leaders at Duke acknowledge that the program may help slow the increase, but don't think it's going to lead to a reduction."

Cautionary Tales of Hidden Costs and Lost Revenue

Hidden costs. In March 2013 Charlie Moran, the CEO of Moran Technology Consulting, shared a potentially jarring scenario with colleagues on the Educause CIO listscrv ("*The potential 'hidden' software cost of running a MOOC class . . .*"). The scenario described significant cost increases in licensing for college data systems as a result of successful MOOC enrollments. Below, reproduced here with his permission, is the potential problem Mr. Moran laid out in his post:

Any school that is teaching a MOOC will potentially add a large subset of the participants to their SIS database for certificate or course credit and future enrollment marketing. If you teach a MOOC but wait until the enrolled students apply for admission to your campus before entering them into your SIS system then this might not be a problem. If you enter students into your SIS because they have a grade or certificate from you and you need to maintain it, then you may have a problem:

- *Most ERP/SIS contracts are based on student headcount or FTE.*

- *Assume your institution has 10,000-student FTE.*

- *Assume your software contracts are based on student FTE.*

- *Assume you paid $1M in license fees for your ERP and you paid $1M in license fees for your database and data warehouse and reporting tools.*

- *Assume that you pay 20% for annual software maintenance for all of this software.*

Then your institution launches a MOOC.

- *For simplicity, assume that you run your MOOC on edX/Udacity/Coursera/etc. at no cost to you.*

Again, in round numbers, assume that 100,000 students enroll in the class, 20,000 complete the course, and 5,000 want a certificate or college credit from your school. The software audit staff at your ERP/DB/Tools vendors contact you about the increase in your FTE, which increased 50% from 10,000 to 15,000. Now, you have to:

- *Pay $500,000 one-time for additional ERP/SIS Licensing*

- *Pay $100,000 more / year FOREVER in an ERP annual maintenance increase*

- *Pay $500,000 one-time for additional Database and other tools Licensing*

- *Pay $100,000 more / year FOREVER in a database and tool annual maintenance increase*

So, for 5,000 additional students, you will pay an additional one-time license cost of $1M and an additional $200,000 / year forever in software maintenance. In general ERP and enterprise-wide DB contract requirements increase with rises in enrollment, but never go down if enrollment falls. A mitigating factor could be that you may charge something for giving a MOOC student a certificate and even more for a grade. Is it enough to pay the one-time fees? Enough to pay the annual maintenance increases?

Moran's numbers are large and clearly dramatic. There are a lot of assumptions in the scenario he lays out and they are based largely on counting MOOC participants as registered students (which does not appear to be happening although there may be a temptation to use MOOCs to inflate enrollment). The financial impact outlined in Moran's scenario will depend on local variables, the numbers of students you add into your SIS, student headcount vs. FTE, and so on. Regardless, it behooves you to review your current contracts to understand the impact that significant, MOOC-generated changes in FTE will have on your budget.

Displaced Income. Large lecture halls filled with hundreds of students and taught by a single faculty member and a few TAs are common. We teach this way not because the model is representative of our best thinking on learning theory and pedagogy but because it makes good economic sense, being an efficient way to manage the costs of delivering lower-level survey courses. The profit from these courses subsidizes the smaller, more intimate (and more marketable) upper-division courses.

When proposing the use of MOOCs to lower costs and increase access, it is critical to contextualize that proposition with this model in mind. You need to assess precisely how your campus pays for your more valued curriculum. Even if you are at a small liberal arts college and you don't offer large lecture hall courses, you must identify how you have structured your business plan to benefit from the current curriculum and how changes to that structure will impact your bottom line.

Agencies across higher education are working to ensure that transferable credits are available to students who participate in MOOCs. As that effort increases, take the opportunity to assess the extent to which that potential financial benefit to students may translate into a loss at your institution. MOOCs, whether provided by you or other institutions, could displace some of your income.

Increased costs. Many hope that MOOCs will reduce the cost of education and increase revenue. Others argue that MOOCs will actually *increase costs*, at least in the short term. Depending on how they are implemented, MOOCs are likely to be layered onto existing institutional commitments as an additional cost rather than replace existing programs. They will require support. By design, they will emphasize active learning, formative assessment, and dynamic content that is easily modified with the appropriate staff support. Enabling data collection to measure learning outcomes in new ways, they will require new systems and staffing models that few campuses are currently prepared to offer. It is possible, even likely, that this could become an outsourced service to which campuses subscribe for a fee.

The private sector is investing heavily in the profitable future they see for education. That investment has altered expectations and encouraged vaguely articulated revenue models. Online learning in various iterations will become more pervasive and viable regardless of whether your campus offers these resources. Take the time to document and identify the trends external to your institution as you assess your internal programs and structures.

Planning Questions:
1. What distinguishes your campus, faculty, and staff? How will you identify (and celebrate and market) and invest in these identified strengths. E.g., invest in professional development for faculty, technologists, librarians, and media specialists.
2. How would MOOCs and online learning offer an opportunity to effect maximum competitive advantage?
3. What gaps in academic support for online learning can you identify?
4. What strategies can you identify to address these gaps

and how will you develop and plan for appropriate staffing?

5. What potential partnerships with other institutions, non-profits, and for-profits can you identify?

6. How will you plan to include stakeholders frequently left out of the strategic planning process, e.g., faculty, staff, and students?

7. How would investments in online learning make sense for your institution at this time?

8. How, specifically, would MOOCs in all their emerging iterations support the mission of the campus?

9. How will you manage revenue sharing with MOOC providers?

10. What impact will participation in MOOCs either as provider or consumer have on your financial plan?

11. To what extent do you leverage income from lower-level courses to subsidize your curriculum?

Chapter 5: Endnotes

26. Green, "Mission, MOOCs, & Money."

27. Kiley, "Nowhere to Turn."

28. Desantis, "A Boom Time for Education Start-Ups."

29. Green, "Mission, MOOCs, & Money."

30. Young, "At South by Southwest Education Event, Tensions Divide Entrepreneurs and Educators."

31. "Coursera Commits to Admitting Only Elite Universities | Inside Higher Ed."

32. Kenneth E. Hartman, "Tips for College Leaders to Make Online Programs Work," *Inside Higher Ed*, February 11, 2013.

31. Young, "Inside the Coursera Contract."

32. Young, "Inside the Coursera Contract."

Michael Nanfito

Chapter 5: Can MOOCs be made to add up? - Recommended Readings

Azevedo, Alisha. "In Colleges' Rush to Try MOOC's, Faculty Are Not Always in the Conversation." *The Chronicle of Higher Education*, September 26, 2012, sec. Technology.

Booker, Ellis. "Can Big Data Analytics Boost Graduation Rates?" *Information Week*, February 5, 2013.

Byerly, Alison. "Before You Jump on the Bandwagon . . ." *The Chronicle of Higher Education*, September 3, 2012, sec. Commentary.

Catropa, Dayna, and Margaret Andrews. "Did MOOCs Just Make Landfall? 10 Questions to Consider." *Inside Higher Ed*, November 5, 2012.

Christensen, Clayton, and Henry J. Eyring. Can Higher Education Be Fixed? The Innovative University, September 23, 2011. http://www.forbes.com/sites/stevedenning/2011/09/23/can-higher-education-be-fixed-the-innovative-university/.

Desantis, Nick. "A Boom Time for Education Start-Ups." *The Chronicle of Higher Education*, March 18, 2012, sec. Technology.

Empson, Rip. "Coursera Takes A Big Step Toward Monetization, Now Lets Students Earn 'Verified Certificates' For A Fee." *TechCrunch*, January 8, 2013.

Green, Kenneth C. "Mission, MOOCs, & Money." *Association of Governing Boards*, February 2013.

Hartman, Kenneth E. "Tips for College Leaders to Make Online Programs Work." *Inside Higher Ed*, February 11, 2013.

Kiley, Kevin. "Moody's Report Calls into Question All Traditional University Revenue Sources." *Inside Higher Ed*, January 17, 2013.

Kim, Joshua. "MOOCS, Online Learning, and the Wrong Conversation." *Inside Higher Ed*, January 2, 2013.

———. "Why MOOCs May Drive Up Higher Ed Costs." *Inside Higher Ed*, March 11, 2013. http://www.insidehighered.com/blogs/technology-and-learning/why-moocs-may-drive-higher-ed-costs.

Kolowich, Steve. "Coursera Strikes MOOC Licensing Deal with Antioch University." *Inside Higher Ed*, October 29, 2012.

———. "Experts Speculate on Possible Business Models for MOOC Providers." *Inside Higher Ed*, June 11, 2012.

———. "How EdX Plans to Earn, and Share, Revenue From Its Free Online Courses." *The Chronicle of Higher Education*, February 21, 2013, sec. Technology.

Korn, Melissa, and Jennifer Levitz. "Online Courses Look for a Business Model." *Wall Street Journal*, January 1, 2013, sec. Small Business.

Lewin, Tamar. "Massive Open Online Courses Prove Popular, If Not Lucrative Yet." *The New York Times*, January 6, 2013, sec. Education.

Makokha, Joseph Maloba. "In Case You Missed It: 'MOOCs, Online Education, and the Library' Report." *Stanford University Libraries*, February 27, 2013.

Mazoue, James G. "The MOOC Model: Challenging Traditional Education." *EDUCAUSE Review*, January 28, 2013.

"Moody's: 2013 Outlook for Entire US Higher Education Sector Changed to Negative." *Moody's Investors Service*, January 16, 2013.

Najar, Nida. "Squeezed Out in India, Students Turn to United States." *The New York Times*, October 13, 2011, sec. World / Asia Pacific.

Nelson, Libby A. "Obama Calls for More Attention to Price, Value, Accreditation in State of the Union." *Inside Higher Ed*, February 13, 2013.

Oblinger, Diana G., and Brian L. Hawkins. "The Myth About Online Course Development." *EDUCAUSE Review*, January 1, 2006.

Pappano, Laura. "Massive Open Online Courses Are Multiplying at a Rapid Pace." *The New York Times*, November 2, 2012, sec. Education / Education Life.

Rivard, Ry. "California Academic Leaders Oppose Outsourcing Plan." *Inside Higher Ed*, March 28, 2013. http://www.insidehighered.com/news/2013/03/28/california-academic-leaders-oppose-outsourcing-plan.

Shirky, Clay. "How to Save College." *The Awl*, February 7, 2013.

Troop, Don. "In a Volatile Economy, Colleges' Endowment Returns Fall Flat." *The Chronicle of Higher Education*, February 1, 2013, sec. Finance.

Watters, Audrey. "Venture Capital and the Future of Open Education: FWK and MOOCs." *Inside Higher Ed*, November 6, 2012.

Young, Jeffrey R. "Coursera Announces Details for Selling Certificates and Verifying Identities." *Wired Campus*, January 9, 2013.

———. "Inside the Coursera Contract: How an Upstart Company Might Profit From Free Courses." *The Chronicle of Higher Education*, July 19, 2012, sec. College 2.0.

———. "New Platform Lets Professors Set Prices for Their Online Courses." *The Chronicle of Higher Education*, December 12, 2012, sec. Technology.

Part 3. The Shape of Things (To Consider)

Chapter 6: **Credible Credits**

At the moment, colleges have a monopoly on the sale of college credits, the only units of learning that can be assembled into credentials with wide acceptance in the labor market. Monopolies are valuable things to control, and monopolists tend not to relinquish them voluntarily. But the MOOC explosion will accelerate the breakup of the college credit monopoly.[35]   —Kevin Carey

How can we create academic assessment and credential programs appropriate to the realities of contemporary learners? And how can we do this without sacrificing the quality and integrity of current models? Answering these questions is vital to dealing with the challenging opportunity confronting agencies concerned with higher education for the twenty-first century. Barriers to accessing traditional higher education—and obstacles to degree completion for students who have successfully matriculated—are adding to the growing pressure to identify viable alternatives to traditional college education. State and federal government officials are drafting legislation requiring public institutions to provide new paths for students struggling to amass required credits to graduate. Badges, fee-based certification, and competency-based education programs are increasingly being scrutinized and—in some cases—adopted. This movement has led to various agencies now creating systems that provide credit for participation in MOOCs and other online learning programs.

The trend toward education persisting over the life and career of a learner, is growing. The contemporary college student is no longer necessarily between the ages of eighteen and twenty two, and few students now complete their college career in four years. Military veterans are seeking college transfer credit for formal and informal training acquired during their service. In the spirit and application of lifelong learning, today's students engage with educational opportunities in a variety of venues inside and outside the formal educational infrastructure. As Cathy Davidson, Professor of Interdisciplinary Studies at Duke University, notes, "People seem to think they know what school is and they know what work is. We live in a world where anyone can learn anything, anytime, anywhere, but we haven't remotely reorganized our workplace or school for this age."[36] Government agencies, influential foundations, and corporate leaders are now actively working on that reorganization.

Digital Badges for Learning: the U.S. Secretary of Education Speaks Out. On September 15, 2011, U.S. Secretary of Education Arne Duncan spoke at the fourth annual launch of the MacArthur Foundation *Digital Media and Lifelong Learning Competition.* In his speech, Duncan referenced the Obama administration plan, "Transforming American Education: Learning Powered by Technology," noting that it "aims to reframe learning as a process that is not only lifelong, but life-wide." Duncan described the persistent reformation of the higher education system as an economic and social imperative, noting that the "cradle-to-career" vision of the Transforming American Education plan is critical to the social and economic development of the nation. Duncan offered remarks about the future of higher education, the importance of innovation, and the value of digital "badges" with respect to documenting and credentialing individual educational accomplishments.[37]

Michael Nanfito

Duncan also acknowledged several agencies working to improve access to education, including the MacArthur Foundation, Mozilla, the University of California Humanities Research Institute, and HASTAC (Humanities, Arts, Science, and Technology Advanced Collaboratory). These groups are all working to provide funding and identify paths to college credit for academic accomplishments outside of the traditional model. Digital badges are a centerpiece of that effort. Badges, Duncan noted, engage, inspire, and serve as acknowledgement of accomplishment in an era of education anywhere and anytime, and as complements to the traditional venues of college and university.

According to Duncan, the participation of schools, corporations, and supporting organizations in the Digital Media and Lifelong Learning Competition "will serve as a catalyst to advance the potential of digital badges. Badges can help engage students in learning, and broaden the avenues for learners of all ages to acquire and demonstrate—as well as document and display—their skills."[38]

Duncan targeted traditional metrics of academic achievement and argued for the development of systems that acknowledge the value of both formal and informal learning. Badges are a critical component of the transition from "credentials that measure seat time to ones that more accurately measure competency" and, he further argued, that shift should be accelerated. Badges, he added, will help measure, document, and communicate knowledge that is acquired by learners in an increasingly interconnected educational matrix in which "learning not only can—but should—happen anywhere, anytime." Digital badges are a mechanism to help universities and colleges acknowledge learning that happens in both "physical and online" environments "and whether learning takes place in schools, colleges or adult education centers, or in afterschool, workplace, military or community settings." The traditional system of schools, colleges, and universities are "very important" points within interconnected "networks of learning." What is required are systems that do a better job of measuring and credentialing learning that occurs in the spaces between these points.

We are witnessing renewed analyses of competency-based education and prior learning assessment. This open and expansive educational model—that of the student actively engaged in the development of learning programs with outcomes measured in their professional development—synchs well with MOOCs and could be a potent combination in the decision-making of learners with respect to their formal education plans and commitments. MOOCs paired with complementary digital badges fit with the trend for twenty-first-century learners to "seek out the right tools among many resources available, and in their fields of interest—and build a record of what they have mastered."

Duncan's remarks highlighted the federal government's commitment to support the cooperative work of traditional education, business, industry, and influential foundations in promoting an increasingly open education infrastructure. "With efforts like this competition, we can encourage breakthroughs in the types of free, high-quality, online Open Educational Resources that lift educational attainment rates and foster renewed economic growth." Harnessing the talent, aspirations, and abilities of new generations of learners and citizens will be key to economic and entrepreneurial renewal, a significant portion of which

Michael Nanfito

is sponsorship of new approaches to providing college credit for knowledge acquired by non-traditional means. To that end, powerful interests are aligning to support the development and acceptance of digital badges.

What then are these badges? How does one acquire them, and from whom?

Digital Badges and the Disintermediation of Credentialing. Digital badges measure competent interaction with material, activities, and peers in a learning environment. Badges as they are implemented today are derived from research into gamification.

In gaming culture and practice, "achievements" (badges, awards, stamps, or challenges) encourage players to do more than simply finish a game: they encourage one to go farther, to explore all aspects of a multi-space environment, and learn what is knowable in the context of that expansive environment.

Achievements/badges are consciously designed into the environment by the developer as specific challenges to be encountered and worked through by the player. Badges are awarded as players successfully navigate the game; they are often interdependent, and build on progress and demonstration of problem solving. Earned badges are visible to the community of participants as part of the player's digital profile. Internet spaces exist for players to post profiles and demonstrate accomplishments. Microsoft's 2005 Xbox Gamerscore system is generally considered to be the first implementation of such an "achievement system." In these multi-game environments, players are motivated to work through challenges and demonstrate accomplishments accrued through demonstration of competency with the entire range of events and challenges across a multi-game environment rather than a single task or activity as part of a single game.

In 2007, two years after Microsoft introduced Xbox Gamerscore, Eva Baker, president of the American Educational Research Association (AERA), stated the need to develop and implement a system of badge-like certifications of student accomplishment. Badges, Baker said, would document learning in formal and informal environments. Building on the achievement systems of gaming environments, learning badges would be public recognition of documented accomplishments and would be visible to universities, employers, and peers.

Despite the call to action by Baker and the AERA, badges failed to get widespread attention. Then, in 2011, Peer 2 Peer University and The Mozilla Foundation, with support from the MacArthur Foundation, co-authored *An Open Badge System Framework*, a white paper conceptualizing badges as an alternative path to certification and credentials for education.

Mozilla, provider of the popular Firefox web browser, develops resources that are open and accessible to everyone. As stated on its website, "Mozilla promotes openness, innovation and opportunity on the Internet by engaging in unique partnerships with some of the world's leading brands and non-profits, as well as with technology, content and service providers." In keeping with that mission, Mozilla's alignment with the MacArthur Foundation and Peer 2 Peer University reflects its intention to put Mozilla's considerable resources behind a plan to develop an open tool to help institutions and organizations authenticate and certify learning.

The white paper outlined a systematic approach to credentialing knowledge and competencies intended to augment the existing model of formal curricula and

Michael Nanfito

degrees. The paper sketches a model in which a student's skills and competencies would be "captured more granularly across many different contexts...collected and associated with online identity and could be displayed to key stakeholders to demonstrate capacities." The paper defined a framework that "outlines the key elements of an open badge system for connected learning contexts, including the badges, associated assessments and an open infrastructure to support issuance, collection and sharing of badges." Badges, the paper reported, would be awarded for competencies regardless of where the competency is developed. A collection of such badges would serve as a "virtual resume of competencies and qualities for key stakeholders such as peers, schools or potential employers." Badges connect the "learning ecology," bridging contexts and making alternative educational channels more "viable, portable, and impactful."[39]

The paper had an impact of its own. In December 2011, the Massachusetts Institute of Technology launched MITx to enable students to take advantage of open online course materials and take online exams to assess their mastery of the material and earn certificates. Foreshadowing— or perhaps reflecting—emerging MOOC participation models, MIT entered into an agreement with OpenStudy, a company that administers online study groups, to issue digital badges to students who consistently provided mentorship and support to colleagues in the online discussion forums supporting the OpenCourseWare project.

Following rapidly on the publication of its 2011 white paper, the Mozilla Foundation staked out its presence as a significant player in the credentialing movement when it announced **Mozilla Open Badges**, a program for creating a common system to issue, earn, and display digital badges across educational environments. That announcement and subsequent software development marked a programmatic commitment to change badges from playful game-based tokens with limited credibility to symbols of certified learning backed by data authenticating students' activities and successes.

On March 14, 2013—two years after Secretary Duncan's speech about digital badges, open educational resources, and credible alternatives to the credentialing of competency and knowledge—Mozilla launched Open Badges 1.0.

Mozilla Open Badges is an online *standard*, an actual tool that institutions and organizations can use to authenticate and verify learning, "making it easy for anyone to issue, earn and display badges across the web— through a shared infrastructure that's free and open to all," as the Mozilla Open Badges website states. Open Badges 1.0 creates a tool that enables organizations to verify competencies for other institutions to review, and for learners to display achievements, interests and skills in an open manner congruent with the online culture and practices of this century. The system is open, enabling students to combine badges from different organizations in a user-managed portfolio that provides a more complete story of individual achievement. Earned badges are controlled by the user and may be displayed for review by others for professional purposes, potential employment or educational programs—as a record of what Secretary Duncan calls "life-wide learning."

Contrary to the image that the label "badge" evokes, digital badges are more than a static emblem. The value of the badge derives from the metadata about the learner's activities and progress relating to the competency for which the badge is issued. Badge metadata includes information about the issuer of the badge along with how, when and why the badge was earned, and links to documents, reviews, and projects associated with the work of the learner. It is a portfolio of progress. As the Open Badges website states, "This supporting data reduces the risk of 'gaming' the system and builds in an implicit validation system. The metadata may vary based on the particular skill, assessment, and issuer." As an integrated system, Open Badges gives users control over display (critical to privacy concerns) and provides tools to manage different displays for different audiences. "Mozilla Backpack," a component of Open Badges, enables users to customize collections of badges for display and review by schools, employers, and universities with details that are relevant to the specific interaction. The backpack gives users an easy way to sort badges by category and display them across such social networking sites as LinkedIn and employers' websites. Open Badges, with supporting resources like the Mozilla Backpack, reflects the sensibilities and intention of a contemporary generation of users.

More than 600 organizations and educational institutions, including Carnegie Mellon University, the University of Illinois at Urbana-Champaign, Empire State College of the State University of New York, NASA, and the Smithsonian Institution, are now using Open Badges to authenticate education and lifelong learning in support of students' education and professional development.

- Mozilla Open Badges is not proprietary — it's free software and an open technical standard. That means any organization can create, issue and verify digital badges, and any user can earn, manage and display these badges all across the web.

- Open Badges knits your skills together. Whether they're issued by one organization or many, badges can build upon each other, joining together to tell the full story of your skills and achievement.

- With Open Badges, every badge is full of information. Each one has important data built in that links back to the issuer, the criteria it was issued under and evidence verifying the credential — a feature unique to Open Badges.

- Open Badges lets you take your badges everywhere. Users now have an easy and comprehensive way to collect their badges in a single backpack, and display their skills and achievements on social networking profiles, job sites, their websites and more.

- Individuals can earn badges from multiple sources, both online and offline. Then manage and share them using the Open Badges backpack. Right now we're launching with the Mozilla backpack — other organizations will be able to use Open Badges to make their own backpacks later this year.

* **Source**: Mozilla's Open Badges Project. MozillaWiki, 2013

Grant funds attached to the Digital Media and Lifelong Learning Competition have attracted institutions eager to experiment with digital badges. The University of Southern California's service-learning division, for example, is among the winners of a MacArthur grant to try the badge platform. According to Susan Harris, the associate director of the Joint Educational Project developed at USC, the project "works with professors to run community-service projects that grant students extra credit for volunteer work. The service-learning community has struggled with how to identify and recognize the outcomes that students learn, like civic knowledge and diversity."[40]

Critics of open badges are concerned that corporations, the federal government, and the "larger educational marketplace" are building an ineffectual system that forces teachers to teach to tests. Some argue that systems like digital badges reduce learning, mastery, and credentials to a cheap facsimile of formal education. Badges, in this view, simply amplify the worst failings of our current educational model in which students are driven from the pursuit of knowledge to chasing after a reward for the sake of the reward rather than the knowledge and mastery it represents.

It is true that significant impetus to explore and implement digital badges comes from corporate and educational entrepreneurs and reformers rather than traditional institutions. The concept and practice of issuing emblems of achievement is well established in commercial information technology sectors. Microsoft and other software development companies, for example, offer online certification programs to help professionals demonstrate competency. The Microsoft Certified Solutions Expert (MCSE) program is a widely recognized model for attaining and demonstrating competency in a complex learning environment. Employers making decisions about staffing and eager to access credentials that provide details about potential employees' academic career, achievements, and competencies have long made use of such digital "badges."

The trend for students to combine formal education with work and professional development will certainly continue. Digital badge systems provide the ability to earn and display emblems of achievement in a structured, portable, and customizable system, and to demonstrate competency without waiting years for a single comprehensive credential. Since few students currently complete a college degree in four years and are increasingly compelled to intersperse education and employment over a longer period of time, such a system may well be attractive and pragmatic for this generation of students. How tools such as digital badges will be accepted and implemented by traditional institutions is yet to be determined. However, it will be difficult to ignore the utility of metadata detailing a student's successes and interests as we all increasingly find ourselves moored in online spaces fueled by social media and open publishing.

Educational leadership has the opportunity and the obligation to actively engage in the dialogue over these 'issues, and to ensure that traditional institutions help direct the course of these emerging trends.

From Badges to Credits. The advent of MOOCs is yet another impetus toward considering the value of issuing, earning, and displaying badges of academic achievement. Similarly, increasing acceptance and implementation of badges will add credence to the argument that MOOCs should be considered for college credit.

Despite concerns that digital badges, alternative assessment models, and open and online learning environments like MOOCs reduce the status of learning to a facsimile of authentic education, many believe that we have arrived at a historic moment in the history of education, and that inevitable changes are on the horizon for higher education policy and programs.

Kevin Carey, director of the education-policy program at the New America Foundation, believes that MOOCs will ultimately (inevitably) be considered for credit. In a September 3, 2012, *Chronicle of Higher Education* article,

Michael Nanfito

he highlights the obvious paradox of MOOCs that do not merit credit despite being taught by prominent scholars from elite schools. Contrasting the current model that enables a "slacker freshman who ekes out a C to collect full credit for a course they barely attend" with the emerging MOOC model in which an enthusiastic, engaged student scores in the top one percent of a "course taught by a world-famous scholar and endorsed by a world-famous university," yet earns no credit, Carey argues that "such cognitive dissonance can't last forever." He goes on to describe scenarios in which accredited colleges will increasingly accept MOOC certificates as transfer credit. He reminds us that there are several thousand accredited schools and that many are struggling to find strategies to enhance their visibility, enrollment, and financial futures. Public officials (as demonstrated in Secretary Duncan's 2011 speech), meanwhile, will continue to press for better access to higher education for families effectively shut out by the current traditional system.[41]

MOOCs in this scenario offer campuses the opportunity to market themselves anew, build (or rebuild) their brand, and boost enrollment numbers in the context of an increasingly inter-networked educational model in which students engage in learning across many venues and over extended time periods. Adhering to a model bound by limited time spent in college (four years), false demographics (18-to-22-year-old students), and one or, at most, two accredited institutions attended, is a failing proposition for campus leadership dealing with older students who have mixed educational backgrounds and various family and employment responsibilities.

When Sebastian Thrun wanted to give his first massive online course away for free, Stanford University had no problem. When he wanted to offer a Stanford-sanctioned certificate to those who completed the course, the university balked. The message is clear. Content and content delivery is negotiable. Sanction of certification and credentialing has been the business and purview of the university.

It is in this context that MOOC providers and other agencies are actively working to certify MOOC participation for credit. An infrastructure to provide for the assessment and credentialing of alternative educational opportunities like MOOCs is gradually taking form. Agencies that have worked for years (and, in some cases, for decades) to verify and recommend alternative courses for credit, and to supervise and proctor exams for credit, are now involved in the validation of emerging online education. Applying well-established and rigorous review programs and protocols to MOOCs likely will confer credibility on these non-traditional learning environments.

The American Council on Education (ACE) and Accredited MOOCs. The American Council on Education (ACE) is leveraging its position as the umbrella agency for higher education in the U.S. to provide leadership in determining the credit-worthiness of MOOCs. ACE College Credit recommendations have long been used to connect workplace learning and formal higher education. Since 1974, the ACE College Credit Recommendations Service has used teams of faculty to review training and educational experiences offered by the military, corporations, and professional associations in order to determine whether they should be issued credit signifying that their learning outcomes are equal to that of traditional, college-level work. ACE institutional membership includes nearly two thousand colleges and universities that use these credit recommendations in their acceptance of credit for courses outside the traditional model. ACE has a client list of over six hundred organizations and institutions for which they evaluate courses and programs. Clients include such companies as Starbucks and McDonald's, such education providers as Skillsoft, and such government agencies as the Federal Aviation Administration. Through the ACE Credit Registry and Transcript System, learners who complete courses with the appropriate credit recommendations can request and obtain transcripts that they can submit to colleges and universities. Approximately 1,200 institutions accept these recommendations for consideration in the credit transfer process. Decisions are made on a case-by-case basis.

In November 2012, ACE announced that it would apply its rigorous credit review process in an evaluation of several MOOCs. Given its long history and successes, ACE is well positioned to influence the acceptance of accreditation for MOOCs. (It is reliably estimated that 82 percent of ACE-endorsed students receive some credit from institutions of higher education because of that recommendation.) By working methodically with various agencies and MOOC providers to develop a comprehensive program for reviewing and credibly accrediting MOOCs, ACE likely will drive traditional colleges and universities to recognize MOOC credits.

Since that 2012 announcement, ACE has evaluated and approved several courses offered by Coursera and Udacity. As ACE president Molly Corbett Broad says on ACE's website, "MOOCs are an intriguing, innovative new approach that holds much promise for engaging students across the country and around the world, as well as for helping colleges and universities broaden their reach. But as with any new approach, there are many questions about long-term potential, and ACE is eager to help answer them—questions such as whether MOOCs can help raise degree completion, deepen college curricula and increase learning productivity."

ACE has considerable foundation support in this effort, including a nearly $900,000 grant from the Bill and Melinda Gates Foundation. With that funding, ACE is going beyond evaluation of specific courses and is establishing research to "identify and answer questions about the disruptive potential of this new and innovative approach to higher education." The agenda for this initiative includes:

- Creation of a Presidential Innovation Lab that will bring together presidents and chancellors from diverse institutions to engage in conversations about potential new academic and financial models, inspired by the disruptive potential of MOOCs, that can help address attainment gaps.

- Evaluation of select Coursera courses for college credit by the ACE College Credit Recommendation Service (ACE CREDIT).

- Examination of effective approaches, pedagogies and practices that lead to student success, as well as the applicability to college degree completion programs of college credit recommendations for MOOCs.

In order to make strategic sense of MOOCs and other emerging online learning initiatives, it is critical to provide spaces for campus leaders to wrestle with their issues and potential. Higher education is grappling with how, when, and to what extent online education will impact existing curricular, pedagogical, administrative and financial models. Ideas like the ACE Presidential Innovation Lab will certainly inspire others to organize similar spaces in the context of their own regional and national consortia. Academic leadership will need such structured programs to effectively grapple with the issues, challenges, opportunities, and institutional obligations related to MOOCs, and to publish outcomes so as to contribute to a disciplined, productive dialog with the broader community of higher education.

Multi-agency collaborations. Many institutions and organizations are working together on developing acceptable paths to credit for participation in MOOCs. In addition to recommending several MOOCs for credit, ACE is collaborating closely with Udacity and San Jose State University in researching the academic rigor and pedagogical implications of MOOCs for low-income students and adult learners. San Jose State, part of the beleaguered California State University system, has committed to persistent review, development, and implementation of alternative online education models. ACE's role in that project is to develop research on the demographics of students who participate in Udacity coursework and to identify effective pedagogical practices, given the demographic and disciplinary context of the courses. This research, undertaken in alliance with the University of Illinois Springfield's Center for Online Learning, Research, and Service, is expected to define attributes that contribute to successful MOOC course completion and will compare demographics within disciplines of students enrolled in both MOOCs and traditional courses.

This may be the kernel of an effective response to criticism of the course-by-course review that ACE typically conducts. If ACE develops an observable methodology that is extensible and easily applied to the MOOC model rather than individual MOOC courses, it could ease the process and accelerate acceptance. The development of such methodologies may influence how MOOCs are developed in the first place, effectively creating a model that responds to documented shortcomings, establishes acceptable online pedagogies, and deepens the penetration of MOOCs and other online programs into higher education. Such work may help articulate better questions for campus leaders as they redefine the nature and shape of higher education in their own institutions. Other organizational efforts to authenticate acceptance of MOOCs, prior learning, and competency-based education include:

The College Board's College Level Examination Program (CLEP), which provides exam-based access to college credit. According to its website, CLEP has been "the most widely trusted credit-by-examination program for over 40 years, accepted by 2,900 colleges and universities and administered in over 1,700 test centers."

Excelsior College, which offers examinations to certify students' understanding of concepts taught in traditional general-education course classrooms, has now extended its portfolio to include MOOCs. "By matching content in MOOCs offered through MIT, Johns Hopkins, Saylor and others to 31 of its existing Excelsior College Examinations (ECE), Excelsior has provided a means for students to demonstrate knowledge gained through the use of free open educational resources such as MOOCs." Ironically, Excelsior College—a pioneer in prior learning—has so far declined to honor ACE credit recommendations for MOOCs. This policy is based on concerns that ACE has moved too quickly to credit MOOCs and that that haste might undermine the work of other organizations working to extend acceptance of prior learning. John Ebersole, the President of Excelsior, is confident that his institution and ACE (which he concedes is the national leader in this space), will ultimately re-converge, as both organizations share the same goals.

The Saylor Foundation is a non-profit organization committed to providing free undergraduate college education "with the goal of producing high course and program completion rates." The foundation does not confer degrees, but offers "the knowledge equivalent of majors in fifteen popular disciplines, and . . . [is] making strides toward providing student credit pathways." Students can use Saylor offerings to prepare for challenge exams that can lead to credit. Saylor and Excelsior College offer a program through which students who complete Saylor online courses can pay a fee to take challenge exams to earn credit via Excelsior, which is a regionally accredited nonprofit online institution.

StraighterLine is another online provider offering low-cost ($99 per month) learning modules that can lead to ACE credit recommendations. StraighterLine has partnered with Excelsior to offer fifteen courses taught by professors. On its website, StraighterLine boldly guarantees that its courses transfer to partner colleges. Agreements with these colleges—almost all online schools—"detail how a StraighterLine course is comparable to and accepted in lieu of a specific course/course requirement at each partner college."

Education Portal, a Silicon Valley-based for-profit, offers over thirty courses that link to challenge exams leading to college credit. Sixteen courses are linked to CLEP, two to Excelsior, and another eight to both exam paths.

In September 2012, Pearson VUE, a subsidiary of the Pearson publishing and education assessment giant, partnered with the edX to offer proctored exams to students participating in edX MOOCs. Previously, edX awarded "certificates of mastery" to the 7,157 graduates of its inaugural MOOC in electrical engineering. Now, as a result of the agreement with Pearson, graduates will receive certificates indicating they passed a proctored exam. Pearson signed a similar agreement with Udacity earlier in 2012. Pearson is almost unique in its capacity to offer a massive, site-based testing infrastructure that can accommodate the scope and scale of emerging massive, open educational models. Such site-based testing could confer additional credibility to credentials earned via MOOCs and certified via proctored exams.

In October 2012, Coursera and Antioch University agreed to license the company's MOOC courses to the university as credit-bearing courses in a bachelor's degree program. Significantly, this is a step for Coursera in the development of a comprehensive course product, for sale to colleges, that integrates content and assessment tools.

In January 2013, Academic Partnerships launched MOOC2Degree, a hybridized collaboration with several of its forty partner institutions. Students entering an online degree program can take the first course in the program as a MOOC, with full course credit offered to those who complete the course. Students moving on in the program will be enrolled in "standard" online courses for full tuition. The MOOC2Degree effort encourages students to get started in full-blown degree programs by lowering the initial threshold. For example, the University of Cincinnati now offers Innovation and Design Thinking as a MOOC. Successful, accredited completion of the course provides the option to embark on Master's degree paths in the university's engineering or business schools. Cleveland State, Florida International, Lamar, and Utah State Universities as well as the Universities of Arkansas, Cincinnati, Texas at Arlington, and West Florida were the first of Academic Partnerships' partner institutions to participate in MOOC2Degree.

Also in January 2013, Georgia State University announced a new policy encouraging its colleges and departments to explore and develop means to grant credit for MOOC courses at other institutions. "The landscape in higher education is changing and Georgia State University is at the forefront," said President Mark Becker in a university press release. "This represents a decision by Georgia State to consider MOOC courses in the way we consider every other course—whether they provide a good education for our students," said George Rainbolt, professor of philosophy and chair of the University Senate Committee on Admissions and Standards. The policy extends current practices in which the university grants course credits to students who take university-vetted examinations, such as the Advanced Placement and International Baccalaureate exams.

Common to all of these developments is the commitment on the part of many agencies and institutions to accept credit for participation in alternative education and improve access to formal degree programs for non-traditional students. This concerted effort speaks directly to the aims of the Obama administration, resonates with persistent political pressure to evaluate educational models based on performance and results, and reflects administrative support for prior learning and competency-based education. The scale and financial strength of these cooperative efforts will almost certainly result in policies and programs favorable to alternative college credit models. Competency-based education and awards for prior learning will find attentive audiences across the higher education landscape and will continue to challenge the tradition of "seat time" as the primary metric of college credentialing. As these programs develop and mature, campus leadership will need to decide whether—or, more likely, to what extent—emerging credentialing models fit with the vision and mission of their institution for students, faculty, and staff.

Planning Questions

1. How can we create academic assessment and credential programs appropriate to the realities of contemporary learners without sacrificing the quality and integrity of current models?
2. How will you evaluate alternative forms of credit?
3. If the "traditional system of schools, colleges, and universities" are in fact critical points "within interconnected 'networks of learning,'" what are the strategic relationships between your institutions and other, emerging or alternative educational opportunities in the matrix available to students?
4. Is your institution prepared to evaluate and, if appropriate, integrate alternative forms of credit?
5. What is your strategy to be actively engaged in the dialogue over these issues, and to ensure that traditional institutions help direct the course of these emerging trends?

Michael Nanfito

Chapter 6 Endnotes

35. Carey, "Into the Future With MOOC's."

36. Young, "'Badges' Earned Online Pose Challenge to Traditional College Diplomas."

37. Duncan, "Digital Badges for Learning."

38. Ibid.

39. Peer 2 Peer University and The Mozilla Foundation, "An Open Badge System Framework: A Foundational Piece on Assessment and Badges for Open, Informal and Social Learning Environments."

40. Young, "'Badges' Earned Online Pose Challenge to Traditional College Diplomas."

41. Carey, "Into the Future With MOOC's."

Michael Nanfito

Chapter 6: Credible Credits - Recommended Readings

"ACE to Assess Potential of MOOCs, Evaluate Courses for Credit-Worthiness." *American Council on Education*, November 13, 2012.

"Coursera Terms of Service." *Coursera*, January 14, 2013. https://www.coursera.org/about/terms.

Duncan, Arne. "Digital Badges for Learning." presented at the 4th Annual Launch of the MacArthur Foundation Digital Media and Lifelong Learning Competition SEPTEMBER 15, 2011, September 15, 2011. http://www.ed.gov/news/speeches/digital-badges-learning.

Empson, Rip. "Coursera Takes A Big Step Toward Monetization, Now Lets Students Earn 'Verified Certificates' For A Fee." *TechCrunch*, January 8, 2013.

Jaschik, Scott. "Admissions Leaders and Legal Experts Debate How to Define Merit." *Inside Higher Ed*, January 18, 2013.

Kolowich, Steve. "American Council on Education Recommends 5 MOOCs for Credit." *The Chronicle of Higher Education*, February 7, 2013, sec. Technology.

Lewin, Tamar. "Public Universities to Offer Free Online Classes for Credit." *The New York Times*, January 23, 2013, sec. Education.

Milliron, Mark David. "Reflections on the First Year of a New-Model University." *The Chronicle of Higher Education*, October 1, 2012, sec. Online Learning.

Mozilla. "Introducing Open Badges 1.0." *The Mozilla Blog*, March 14, 2013. http://blog.mozilla.org/blog/2013/03/14/open_badges/.

Nelson, Libby A. "Did State of the Union Create Opening for Competency-based Programs and Other Innovations?" *Inside Higher Ed*, February 14, 2013.

New, Jake. "Mozilla Releases Long-Discussed Software to Offer 'Badges' for Learning." The Chronicle of Higher Education. *The Wired Campus*, March 14, 2013.

Pannapacker, William. "Cultivating Partnerships in the Digital Humanities." *Chronicle of Higher Education*, May 13, 2013.

Peer 2 Peer University, and The Mozilla Foundation. "An Open Badge System Framework: A Foundational Piece on Assessment and Badges for Open, Informal and Social Learning Environments." University of California Humanities Research Institute, March 1, 2011.

Rees, Jonathan. "Essays on the Flaws of Peer Grading in MOOCs." *Inside Higher Ed*, March 5, 2013.

Tilsley, Alexandra. "Dartmouth to End Use of Advanced Placement Scores for Credit." *Inside Higher Ed*, January 18, 2013.

Young, Jeffrey R. "American Council on Education May Recommend Some Coursera Offerings for College Credit." *The Chronicle of Higher Education*, November 13, 2012, sec. Technology.

———. "'Badges' Earned Online Pose Challenge to Traditional College Diplomas." *The Chronicle of Higher Education*, January 8, 2012, sec. College 2.0.

Chapter 7: **MOOCs and the Measurement of Knowledge and Competency**

The emergence of MOOCs has been and will continue to be a catalyst for more discussions among presidents, provosts, trustees, deans, accrediting agency officials, and others about the quality of MOOC courses, the value of MOOC certificates, and the potential threat that MOOCs offered by elite institutions and their partners like Coursera and Udacity might pose to other segments and sectors.[42]

—Casey Green

In 2012, Pepperdine University provost Darryl Tippens penned a thoughtful *Chronicle of Higher Education* essay in defense of the value of residential liberal arts colleges in response to popular enthusiasm for "distance learning." While declaring the value of liberal education, Tippens noted the extreme variations in higher education in the U.S.: "Higher education is not a single industry producing a single 'product,' but an extremely varied enterprise, with more than 4,000 institutions doing different things in different ways, with different ends in mind. The confusion shows up in the debates about whether technology (specifically, distance learning) will 'save' us."[43]

Tippens went on to declare that "reflection and practice together are the best pedagogy." The togetherness he referenced is the *actual*, face-to-face gathering of people in synchronous time and space. He also acknowledged that interest in MOOCs was driven in part by faults with the current system of higher education, and concerns of taxpayers called upon to cover its costs. "Anything as sprawling and complex as higher education means that something, somewhere, is being done poorly or flat wrong. Too many professors, schooled in the finest research universities in the world, have learned to scorn teaching and even to view undergraduates as impediments to their professional advancement . . . No wonder some people think that education can be standardized, easily packaged, and cheaply distributed. No wonder taxpayers are less willing to finance the enterprise. As in Hamlet, we are hoist with our own petard."[44]

In response, Clay Shirky pointed out in a February 2013 essay, "How to Save College," that Pepperdine students can secure both masters and doctorate degrees from the University while enrolled in its online learning programs. Shirky, to expand on Tippens's Shakespearian theme, would have us believe that the Pepperdine provost doth protest too much.[45]

Tippens' essay and Shirky's response provide an opening to ask more interesting questions about the future of education, the nature of measuring competency, and how hybridized learning spaces of in-person seminars and online essays and exchanges can be explored, developed, and implemented.

As Shirky argues elsewhere in his response, MOOCs and online education have arrived during a time when students and their parents—given economic realities and the finite capacity of the traditional model—are open to new options. Higher education in the U.S. is not a single industry with a single product line. Rather, it is a complex hybridization of intent and implementation loosely held together by adherence to policies and oversight inherited from a previous century. The traditional and the online are destined to blend and coexist rather than battle for market share until one or the other dies off.

Michael Nanfito

Leadership in all sectors of higher education must take a stance and work together to craft a newly durable model for higher education.

Education as an organized institutional effort evolves and is responsive to cultural and technological developments, just as does any other sector of society. There is nothing sacred about the structure or the administration of the college or university. Organizational design is a tool we use to facilitate the stated objectives of the institution. Metrics of value and accomplishment are reshaped and sharpened as increasingly sophisticated tools become more readily available and require less training to implement and use.

In this context, MOOCs put questions about the measurement of academic achievement, scholarship and scholarly communication front and center.

Calls for the clarification of what is known and knowable at the completion of students' college and university careers are on the increase. Measuring academic accomplishment with the metric of "seat time" and the credit hour is losing purchase. Tools to monitor progress and accomplishment in online learning environments (derivative of similar demands in business and industry) are under development and in some cases already implemented. As Carol Geary Schneider, President of the Association of American Colleges and Universities said, "Clearly, we need a new system that can demonstrate whether students are gaining proficiency in applying their learning to complex, unscripted problems and new settings."[46]

Credit hours and competency: contextualizing the issues and opportunities. In December 2012, the Carnegie Foundation announced that it would consider alternatives to the century-old credit hour as the unit of measure in higher education. The credit hour (a synthesis of the Carnegie Unit and the Student Hour) is the academic currency used by American colleges and universities to measure academic achievement. Although originally implemented in 1906 to provide a standard of eligibility for, and access to, pensions for college professors, the credit hour has come to measure and inform far more than that. A measure for time spent in a class setting and interaction between faculty and student, it now provides structure and metrics to huge swaths of the business of academe, including the workloads of faculty and students, degree requirements, and student financial aid.

The credit hour was implemented in an era of great expansion of the traditional campus, as more colleges and universities with more classrooms and more seats in more cities opened up across the country. We are now in a different era—one of expanding virtual curricula and courses with no seats and limited student contact with faculty in the traditional manner. The rise of MOOCs and other iterations of online learning programs, with little or no emphasis on traditional classroom participation, intensifies the debate over learning metrics that do not measure instructional time spent in non-existent seats in non-existent classrooms.

Schools with online education programs need appropriate systems for assessing learning and academic achievement in the online environment, and to devise such a system while still appropriately valuing and measuring learning wrought by the talented and caring faculty cited by Tippens. It is no less challenging to find a way to sever the link, where appropriate, between the century-old credit hour, tied to seat time, and student access to financial aid for courses in which there is no seat time.

Michael Nanfito

In a 2006 article titled, "No College Left Behind?" Doug Lederman of *Inside Higher Ed* crystallized this issue and its history. Lederman noted that Charles Miller, then chairman of the Commission on the Future of Higher Education, called for colleges and universities to do a better job of measuring knowledge acquired by students and sharing assessed results with the public. Miller had declared that tools were available to measure academic achievement and student learning. "We need to assure that the American public understand through access to sufficient information, particularly in the area of student learning, what they are getting for their investment in a college education," Miller wrote in a memo sent to fellow commission members. Similarly, Patrick Callan, president of the National Center for Public Policy and Higher Education, was quoted as saying, "Higher education has deflected the idea for the past quarter century by arguing that the kinds of things we want undergraduate education to teach are not really measurable." Callan acknowledged the concerns of administrators and faculty on the ground: "There's been this idea that we'll just pull some standardized test off the shelf, resulting in a dumbing down of what higher education means."[47]

Faculty and campus leaders worried then—and continue to worry—that a federally mandated metric for academic success, applied equally to online learning programs, universities, colleges, community colleges, and across a student population ranging from the traditional 18-22-year-old to adult learners balancing full-time jobs and education, must necessarily fail. In opposition to sweeping mandates and national approaches, Stanley N. Katz, Princeton University professor and former president of the American Council of Learned Societies, warned of the negative impact of sweeping federal policies implementing a common standard across American higher education. Katz cautioned, "Either there won't be agreement, and it will be overly controversial, or it will be reduced to an elastic, lowest common denominator, as in No Child Left Behind, in which case it will become trivial."[48]

Polarization among prominent figures in higher education notwithstanding, work on new approaches to assessment has progressed. In 2011, the Lumina Foundation released the *Degree Qualifications Profile*. Written by four authorities on assessment and student learning (Clifford Adelman of the Institute for Higher Education Policy, Peter Ewell of the National Center for Higher Education Management Systems, Paul Gaston of Kent State University, and Carol Geary Schneider of the American Association of Colleges & Universities), the *DQP* was intended to "help transform U.S. higher education." The framework provided in the document sought to clarify parameters regarding "what students should be expected to know and be able to do once they earn their degrees—at any level." The *DQP* outlines five learning outcomes "critical for all academic programs in higher education," represented on a graphic depiction of the framework called the "Degree Profile Spiderweb":

1. Applied learning is used by students to demonstrate what they can do with what they know.

2. Intellectual skills are used by students to think critically and analytically about what they learn, broadening their individual perspectives and experiences.

3. Specialized knowledge is the knowledge students

demonstrate about their individual fields of study.

4. Broad knowledge transcends the typical boundaries of students' first two years of higher education, and encompasses all learning in broad areas through multiple degree levels.

5. Civic learning is that which enables students to respond to social, environmental and economic challenges at local, national and global levels.

"As students progress through higher education, earning associate, bachelor's and master's degrees, their knowledge, skills and abilities in each of the five areas of learning grow. Like the spiral threads of a spider web, the profile for each degree level grows outward as each builds upon the one before it, and supports those that follow."[49]

As it turned out, Katz's warnings about a sweeping plan with national scope failing to gain traction had merit. In 2013, two years after the release of the *Degree Qualifications Profile*, Peter Ewell, one of the primary authors, drafted a follow-up report. The follow-up tacitly acknowledged that the *DQP* was not generally accepted or understood, much less implemented. Schneider wrote candidly in the Afterword to Ewell's report about the challenges the *DQP* faces in calling for a more "organized and strategic campaign if colleges and universities are to be more intentional and more effective in graduating students who are demonstrably well prepared for work, for civic responsibility, and for realizing their hopes for a better life." Schneider outlined some specific challenges including lack of agreement among "influential leaders" as to the benefits of the framework, campus resistance to assessment, and the reality that the persistence of colleges as "a set of separate, discrete, and even 'siloed' units—individual courses, the majors, general education, the co-curriculum, and so on—works at cross-purposes to the DQP's conception of a more intentional and, ultimately, integrative educational experience."[50]

In support of the "intentionality" of the original framework, Ewell exhorts faculty and administrators to "develop consistent and systematic ways to gather evidence that the competencies the DQP describes are actually being mastered at the levels claimed." The follow-up report and Schneider's reasoned Afterword offer more specific examples of how to make effective use of the framework, and are well worth review and discussion at the campus level.

In the meantime, direct assaults on the credit hour have persisted. In September 2012, Amy Laitinen, deputy director for Higher Education at the New America Foundation, issued *Cracking the Credit Hour*, a report arguing that the extension of the credit hour beyond its original intent is the source of many of the problems in higher education today. The report raises several examples of why the traditional metric is flawed and should be replaced, including:

- Limitations to acceptance of transfer credits by institutions themselves.

- Grade inflation.

- Failure of a model that measures seat time and classroom participation in an era of increasing online education.[51]

Carol Geary Schneider had it right. In her Fall 2012 *Liberal Education* essay, "Is It Finally Time to Kill the Credit

Hour?" Schneider makes a persuasive case that we are very far from a coherent national plan. In light of that reality, taking the opportunity to review examples of existing competency-based learning programs is time well spent. "We need to take the time and learn from the assessment experiments that are going on all over higher education. We also need to build broad and compelling agreement on what twenty-first-century markers of student accomplishment actually look like. And, soberingly, that work is still in draft form."[52]

Models for Review and Consideration. Competency-based education is not new. Examining the development and attributes of programs currently in place will be critical to understanding their relationship to emerging online education, curricular development, and the roles of faculty and learner. Most important, such a review will provide context for making informed strategic decisions about MOOCs and online education at your campus.

Some interesting models include the Western Governors University, founded in 1997 by nineteen state governors, which has been steadily developing and extending a program of online degree offerings for over a decade; Southern New Hampshire University, which more recently made significant strides in implementing new models accommodating the needs and academic ambitions of contemporary learners; and—fully a quarter century before the founding of WGU—Alverno College and Empire State College, which began developing bold approaches to ability-based learning assessment. In order to properly study the question of whether or not, or to what extent, to implement competency-based programs, we need to review established ones, including their intellectual, pedagogical, technical, and policy frameworks. The following brief review of examples will highlight what can be accomplished after hard and honest evaluation of institutional strategy and educational opportunity.

Alverno College. The roots of competency-based education stem from traditional face-to-face learning in brick-and-mortar campuses. In 1973, after nine years of focused development, Alverno College launched its *Competence Based Learning* program. The new program had at its core the idea of "teaching students to learn, internalize, and then externalize and apply knowledge gained in the classroom to their life and their workplace."[53] The genesis and development of the program is recounted in the July 1985 *Alverno Magazine*: "Beginning in 1964 and continuing through 1969, the Alverno administration recognized the impact that rapid changes in technology, the economy, politics and sociological shifts were having on the process of educating college students. The complexities of modern society were eroding away the effectiveness of traditional teaching techniques that had been used for centuries."

Keenly aware of the impact of these changes, Alverno administration scheduled a three day workshop for faculty and students to review and (eventually) rebuild "Curriculum integration and reorganization, the traditional grading system and the learning process itself." In support of this effort a "new academic planning committee was developed to analyze and make recommendations based on all of the data collected at the meetings."[54]

This description of the forces encouraging development of Alverno's program would sound familiar to all of us forty years later. Significantly, the hallmarks of the program (as it has evolved since 1973) closely resemble components of

Michael Nanfito

the MOOC model that incorporates programmatic systems enabling assessment, feedback, and individual performance data.

In support of the transformative program, Alverno worked to develop specific components, assessment, and support models. As described in "Out of Crisis, Opportunity" (From *Reform of General Education to Transformation: Creating a Culture of Learning*, Alverno College Institute, 2009), "The core of Alverno's new curriculum model would consist of eight abilities, experiential learning, mastery and assessment . . . Assessment and the eight ability levels would become the means for determining the depth of understanding and learning a student experienced while at Alverno College...." What most clearly distinguishes Alverno's learning process and assessment from testing is best described in the following quote from Sister Austin Doherty: "Because assessment focuses on the application of abilities, students learn to tie knowledge, theory, motivation and self-perception to constructive action. They discover early that assessment is not a concluding step to learning; it is a natural part of every learning step we take." In essence, each assessment concludes one step in the learning process while beginning the next.

In order to "bridge the gap between the classroom and practical application within the workplace and community," the college fostered a culture of self-evaluation culminating in individual demonstration of competency and learning outcomes based on a common currency expressed in the *Eight Abilities*:

Communication makes meaning of the world by connecting people, ideas, books, media and technology.

You must demonstrate and master the ability to speak, read, write and listen clearly, in person and through electronic media.

Analysis develops critical and independent thinking. You must demonstrate and master the ability to use experience, knowledge, reason and belief to form carefully considered judgments.

Problem Solving helps define problems and integrate resources to reach decisions, make recommendations or implement action plans. You must demonstrate and master the ability to determine what is wrong and how to fix it, working alone or in groups.

Valuing approaches moral issues by understanding the dimensions of personal decisions and accepting responsibility for consequences. You must demonstrate and master the ability to recognize different value systems, including your own; appreciate moral dimensions of your decisions and accept responsibility for them.

Social Interaction facilitates results in group efforts by eliciting the views of others to help formulate conclusions. You must demonstrate and master the ability to elicit other views, mediate disagreements and help reach conclusions in group settings.

Developing a Global Perspective requires understanding of -- and respect for -- the economic, social and biological interdependence of global life. You must demonstrate and master the ability to appreciate economic, social and ecological connections that link the world's nations and people.

Effective Citizenship involves making informed choices and developing strategies for collaborative involvement in community issues. You must demonstrate and master the ability to act with an informed awareness

Michael Nanfito

of issues and participate in civic life through volunteer activities and leadership.

Aesthetic Engagement integrates the intuitive dimensions of participation in the arts with broader social, cultural and theoretical frameworks. You must demonstrate and master the ability to engage with the arts and draw meaning and value from artistic expression.

Based on local experience as well as inter-institutional collaborations in project teams and as consultants, Alverno faculty and administrators developed an empirical analysis of successful student transformation, identifying "how and when students' learning is most strongly a product of their curricula." Three "stances" or "postures" inform the process:

1. The more local study and evaluation of teaching and learning, particularly at the course and department level that are part of any ongoing educational enterprise in a particular place.

2. The periodic program and institutional evaluations that are part of both formal accreditation and special larger evaluative projects, in which outside or external information begin to inform practice.

3. And finally, and perhaps most significantly, a more comprehensive scholarship of teaching and learning in relationship to institutional culture in general, where we learn from our own studies and those of colleagues at other institutions and bring those findings back to inform analyses of questions on our campus.

In *Learning That Lasts* (Mentkowski & Associates, 2000), Alverno College articulated these three postures as *standing in, standing beside*, and *standing aside* the educational practice of the college:

Standing in: *Developing an integrated understanding of what kinds of learning frameworks, strategies, and structures work at one's own campus, arrived at through analyses of practice and campus documentation.*

Standing beside: *A continuing analysis of practice in partnership with other institutions that can shape one's own transformational acts and guidelines of institutional transformation.*

Standing aside: *Tailoring literature and practice review to specific campus issues.*

Alverno's curriculum enables faculty to thoroughly document individual student accomplishment, using common assessment tools and persistent feedback. Echoing the intent to position Alverno graduates to be successful citizens, the program is established to parallel the workings of the "real world." Grades are eschewed. Mastery of content is demonstrated and acknowledged in narrative transcripts detailing the individual assessment of each student. More recently, Alverno has developed a **Diagnostic Digital Portfolio** (DDP) to provide an effective and manageable process for this program.

The DDP supports Alverno's ability-based program *as an integral component of the curriculum*, not an afterthought or an add-on. Prefiguring some of the attributes of digital badge metadata, it provides accessible performance data enabling the student to follow learning progress throughout her career at Alverno. It helps process feedback from faculty and peers, and provides viewable patterns of academic work to ensure students' control of their development and encourage development of authorized and autonomous learners. The DDP is designed to measure key "performances" in students' work. Designed and activated by faculty, they may include activities,

Michael Nanfito

assignments, and assessments to be completed by each student as an integral part of degree performance. Within the DDP, each performance contains criteria and feedback critical to the self-assessment that is a hallmark of the program. Students use the system to review and document progress across courses and the "eight abilities," and to set goals for further learning. The DDP provides a window into students' work for faculty to view and assess progress, and to provide feedback and commentary on observed patterns of performance. The commentary informs student goal-setting and faculty mentoring. Ongoing course curriculum development relies on aggregate data from student portfolios to evaluate program objectives and outcomes. In this way, the curriculum of Alverno College undergoes continuous review and renewal.

The components of the Alverno College curriculum and supporting systems anticipate the development and implementation of online competency-based programs and MOOCs. The DDP is a practical tool to be evaluated by any school interested in the potential of actual tools used in facilitating online learning with competency-based elements. Alverno has made a version of the portfolio available for other institutions to use. DDP (v 3.2), available for download from the Alverno College website, is customizable; other institutions can define the assessment matrices they wish to use and how the developmental levels are to be defined.

Alverno College works in various collaborative ways to assist other schools in defining competency-based programs of their own. Since 1980, the college has hosted the Institute for Educational Outreach to share its approach to competency-based education.

Statement from the President of Alverno College

In the best interest of students – who will one day be future leaders – effective teaching needs to go beyond the simple presentation of information. That is why for more than 40 years, Alverno College has been committed to ability-based curriculum design and the assessment-as-learning approach to education. Alverno's curriculum requires all students to master, within the disciplines, what the faculty has developed as eight core abilities critical to the worlds of work, family and civic community. These abilities include communication, analysis, problem solving, valuing in decision-making, social interaction, developing a global perspective, effective citizenship and aesthetic engagement.

Integral to students' mastery of Alverno's abilities is a rigorous and individualized assessment process involving observation and judgment of each student's performance. Students are taught to self-assess their performance based on public criteria. Feedback from faculty acts as a mirror, providing students with matter for both reflection and growth while raising questions that enable students to critique and further develop their abilities and ideas. This assessment process takes learning one step further—from knowledge to performance, from thought to action, from belief to practice.

Technology presents opportunities to enhance this learning process in amazing new ways. Alverno has introduced hybrid courses that blend the benefits of online and classroom learning. While the delivery mode is different, these courses remain rooted in our pedagogical belief that students should be active learners who effectively demonstrate they have learned the subject matter.

To preserve the abilities-based curriculum and assessment-as-learning approach in this new format, Alverno

Michael Nanfito

faculty members attend intense, specialized training before teaching hybrid courses. This training assists faculty in developing performance-based assessments of the abilities in a hybrid format. In addition, the training guides them in developing meaningful communication and collaboration between students and faculty and among students to ensure effective delivery of the feedback that is so critical to Alverno's learning process.

Because we expect constant learning and improvement from our students, it's only fair that we ask the same of ourselves. That is why we constantly strive to find new ways to explore teaching with technology while staying true to our unique curriculum. We intentionally consider not only content but competency and encourage others to do the same. It is the through assessment of defined abilities that education becomes a model of the real world, where learning comes from engaging in complex tasks, versus simply reading about them.

Dr. Mary J. Meehan
President, Alverno College

SUNY Empire State. On March 19, 2013, the State University of New York (SUNY) board of trustees announced a bold vision outlining how prior-learning assessment, competency-based programs, and MOOCs will inform a plan to ensure that students complete degrees on time and for reduced cost. According to the announcement, the new initiative—*Open SUNY*—will "bring all online courses offered at each of the system's 64 campuses onto a shared and comprehensive online environment, making them accessible to all of the system's 468,000 students and 88,000 faculty."[55]

Significantly, the pre-existing prior-learning assessment

and competency-based programs of SUNY's Empire State College will serve as the mechanism driving the initiative. Nancy L. Zimpher, SUNY chancellor, cited SUNY Empire State College's expertise in this area as the foundation for the system-wide initiative: "The prior-learning expertise at Empire State would make it possible for the New York system to undertake the new effort."

What is it about Empire State that is relevant to the development and implementation of successful online learning programs, and how does this relate to our MOOC discussion? Much like Alverno College, Empire State College was born of the educational innovations of the 1960s and 1970s. Founded in 1971, by Ernest Boyer, Empire State forged processes and programs to provide alternative paths to higher education for students outside the mainstream including "forgoing classes in favor of independent and group studies; rejecting traditional disciplinary departments; eschewing grades for narrative evaluations; and, with faculty mentors working with learners individually, devising unique and personalized degree programs that incorporated learning acquired beyond the academy. Unlike prescribed curricula and course outlines, co-developed learning contracts presumed that learners had unique goals and interests and were active partners in the design of their own learning."[56]

The Council on Adult and Experiential Learning (CAEL) website defines prior learning as "learning gained outside a traditional academic environment."[57] Prior learning is acquired through living one's life and includes (but is not limited to) work experience, training programs, military service, independent study, non-credit courses, volunteer or community service, travel, and non-college courses and seminars. The Empire State model recognizes that traditional academic accomplishments are but one component of the continuum of education, and that this "prior learning" is relevant to the development of the whole person. Fundamental to the Empire State program is the acknowledgement that some of an individual's prior learning represents college-level knowledge and thus should be assessed and credentialed as part of the degree completion process.

Like mainstream colleges and universities, Empire State recognizes that the institutional experience is a significant driver in educating individuals and creating engaged citizens, and that the successful acquisition of a college degree is a hugely important milestone in this quest. Minimizing barriers to reaching that milestone is an important tenet of Empire State. (This is not to reduce college to a "milestone," but rather to place it on an experiential trajectory.) In this context, creation of a programmatic approach to assessing and awarding credit for prior learning helps to minimize redundancy, and reduce what is perceived to be unnecessary time and cost in attaining a degree.

As noted in Chapter 6, assessing and awarding credit for prior learning is not new and is not exclusive to schools like Empire State College. Institutions participate in a cooperative network of learning environments that include traditional schools, colleges, universities, and credentialing oversight from agencies like the American Council on Education (ACE). As Benke, Davis, and Travers note in "SUNY Empire State College: A Game Changer in Open Learning, there are a variety of means at the disposal of all institutions to recognize prior learning: "Credit for prior learning can be awarded based on a number of assessment options. These include training or exams that have been pre-evaluated through outside organizations, such as the American Council on Education (ACE), through the college's own evaluation, or through an individualized prior learning assessment process."[58]

The cooperative network facilitating assessment and credentialing across institutional boundaries may be viewed as part of the "unbundling" process that many predict will impact higher education. This unbundling—specifically separation of the acquisition of knowledge from institutional credentialing of that acquisition—has been the topic of much discussion and debate, especially with the advent of online learning and MOOCs. On one level, institutions already agree that it is acceptable to credential a graduate who has not received his or her entire college education from a single college or university; colleges have long accepted some percentage of transfer credits in the credential process. At this point, we may be dickering about the scope and the scale of that process.

Unbundling knowledge and the college credential: look to the past to decipher the future. In 1981, William K.S. Wang, in "The Dismantling of Higher Education," outlined a bundle of five core services provided to students by traditional colleges and universities, including imparting information, counseling, credentialing, "coercion," and "club membership." Wang suggested how elements of these services might be provided by alternative means and agencies. With respect to *imparting information* and *credentialing,* two services pertinent to this review, Wang described how the traditional institution provides information and knowledge via classroom lecture, traditional texts, and the library. Wang proposed that the unbundled model would provide information via *hired lectures, commercial tutoring firms,* and *commercially*

Michael Nanfito

developed course materials. He also suggested that credentialing would be managed and delivered via external credentialing agencies that would assign and grade papers, develop and grade examinations, and assess progress towards the degree.[59]

In 1981, Wang could not see (or perhaps he could) the future developments of the "adjunctification" of faculty, MOOCs, and the policy decisions of agencies like ACE reviewing and certifying MOOC courses for credit—all developments that reflect much of his thinking. MOOCs and online education are part of a long, persistent progression of educational and institutional change.

In her 2013 "Unbundling . . . and Reinforcing the Hierarchy?", Margaret Andrews noted that Wang's article foreshadowed some of what is happening now as networked technology and the agencies and corporations that support and provide it are increasingly integrated into the provision of the college and university experience. Andrews notes that, unlike the environment in 1981, higher education now has an expansive for-profit sector, student access to internet and web services and applications, interest in the development of badges and certificates, and continued work on how to award credit and credentials.

At Empire State College, this unbundling and the assessment of prior learning sets the stage for programmatic development of personalized degree programs that mesh broad guidelines for majors, the academic and professional aspirations of the student, and the body of knowledge the student brings to the college experience. Students and assigned faculty mentors collaborate to create individualized programs that lead to degrees representing successful completion of requirements outlined in the major. Students share responsibility and accountability for their education as co-creators of the program. As at Alverno College, consciously connecting the educational program to the student's life in a comprehensive manner is designed into the system.

That system of individual review and student accountability is supported by the learner's portfolio. The e-Portfolio at Empire State is used by the faculty-mentor and the student to reflect, assess, recommend, and plan an unfolding educational program. Faculty and learners both contribute to the narrative in the portfolio; the process results in a partnership of assessment and accountability, and aggregated data from student portfolios contributes to a continuous curricular review process.

As Benke, Davis, and Travers explain, "Within this personal degree plan, a learner can design individualized, independent studies in partnership with an appropriate faculty mentor, either face-to-face or online. Learners are expected to be active partners in the design of the learning contract associated with any study, with the faculty mentor acting as a learning coach, posing questions, and helping the learner think through the issues." The students have more "skin in the game" in this model, and with increased authority comes accountability and a new authenticity that is integral to their future: "In the college's mentor-learner model, learners examine what they have learned, where they want to go in their education, and what it takes to get there. Learners note that although the degree planning and prior learning assessment processes are difficult, they develop self-awareness as learners and the capacity to continue their learning in work and other educational settings." This expansive faculty role is key to the development of the learning-centered university.

Lessons from Learning-Centered Institutions. The

Michael Nanfito

decades-long trajectory and evolution of the institutions profiled here illustrate successful transformation from learner-centered to *learning*-centered organizations. The former successfully move the learner to the center of the process but retains the traditional boundaries and barriers between faculty and learners. The latter move *learning* to the center. The faculty-learner dynamic is changed, becoming less hierarchical and more concentric in structure and intent around the real objective—learning. Significantly, these institutions have fully integrated metrics for prior learning and competency into the curricular programs proper, rather than including them as add-ons or afterthoughts. A culture of assessment and curricular review, supported by organizational and systemic tools, permeates the operations and academic work of students and faculty.

This is the interesting connection to MOOCs— particularly those developed and implemented by faculty like Siemens and Downes in the connectivist mode.

Alverno College and Empire State College developed themselves as learning organizations—inherently reflective and collaborative—effectively altering their institutional DNA. The interactive, participatory design of the MOOC as designed and delivered by Siemens and Downes has a great deal in common with the faculty-mentor/learner partnerships in these open colleges. Students in both models are required to take active responsibility for the shape of their education. The systems implemented to facilitate assessment of student progress provide a comprehensive narrative of knowledge gained and competency with the materials in the student's coursework. The measurement of knowledge and competency in open education environments and MOOCs requires active utility of these achievement systems. Alverno and Empire State demonstrate that metrics of academic accomplishment need not rely on seat time and credit hours. Whatever one may think about open education, there are lessons to be learned from these institutions about the mechanics of collaboration and innovation. In response to Carol Geary Schneider's call to explore success stories in this mode, reviewing these structures and functions will help any campus working to make strategic sense of MOOCs, online learning, and open educational resources.

MOOCs and the competency-based educational models of these institutions share another attribute: they make use of systems that collect a great deal of information about students' activities and progress. The achievement systems of Alverno and Empire State are rich repositories of information helping mentors and students analyze and adapt to outcomes in the learning environment. Similarly, commercial MOOC providers are also developing, or collaborating to deliver, data collection systems designed to gather and store massive amounts of information about what students study, when and for how long they do so, while tracking the scope and timeline of their academic progress. "Big data," as it is known, is fast becoming big business, and is advertised as a powerful learning analytic tool. Learning analytics and adaptive learning—and the evaluation of the technologies and services supporting them—will necessarily be part of your review of online learning and MOOCs.

Chapter 7 Endnotes

42. Green, "Mission, MOOCs, & Money."

43. Tippens, "Technology Has Its Place."

44. Ibid.

45. Shirky, "Your Massively Open Offline College Is Broken."

46. Schneider, "Is It Finally Time to Kill the Credit Hour?".

47. Lederman, "No College Left Behind?".

48. Ibid.

49. Adelman et al., "The Degree Qualifications Profile."

50. Ewell et al., "The Lumina Degree Qualifications Profile (DQP): Implications for Assessment."

51. Laitinen, "Cracking the Credit Hour."

52. Schneider, "Is It Finally Time to Kill the Credit Hour?".

53. "History of the Alverno Learning Process: Introduction," http://depts. alverno.edu/archives/alphistory/

54. Ibid.

55. Doyle, "SUNY Board Outlines Implementation of Open SUNY."

56. Benke, Davis, and Travers, "Chapter 11: SUNY Empire State College: A Game Changer in Open Learning."

57. "CAEL - Prior Learning Assessment Services."

58. Benke, Davis, and Travers, "Chapter 11: SUNY Empire State College: A Game Changer in Open Learning."

59. Wang, "The Dismantling of Higher Education."

Michael Nanfito

Chapter 7: MOOCs and the Measurement of Knowledge and Competency - Recommended Readings

Berrett, Dan. "Carnegie, the Founder of the Credit-Hour, Seeks Its Makeover." *The Chronicle of Higher Education*, December 5, 2012, sec. Curriculum.

Bourbon, Julie. "Different Approaches to Online Education | Association of Governing Boards." *Trusteeship*, February 2013.

Bowen, William G., Matthew M. Chingos, Kelly A. Lack, and Thomas I. Nygren. "Interactive Learning Online at Public Universities: Evidence from Randomized Trials." Ithaka S+R, May 22, 2012.

Brooks, David. "The Campus Tsunami." *The New York Times*, May 3, 2012, sec. Opinion.

Byerly, Alison. "Essay on How MOOCs Raise Questions About the Definition of Student." *Inside Higher Ed*, October 29, 2012.

Duncan, Arne. "Digital Badges for Learning." presented at the 4th Annual Launch of the MacArthur Foundation Digital Media and Lifelong Learning Competition SEPTEMBER 15, 2011, September 15, 2011.

Ewell, Peter, George Kuh, Stanley Ikenberry, and Carol Geary Schneider. "The Lumina Degree Qualifications Profile (DQP): Implications for Assessment." National Institute for Learning Outcomes Assessment, January 2013.

Fain, Paul. "The Credit Hour Causes Many of Higher Education's Problems, Report Finds." *Inside Higher Ed*, September 5, 2012.

Fishman, Rachel. "State U Online | NewAmerica.net." *New America Foundation*, April 23, 2013.

Green, Kenneth C. "Mission, MOOCs, & Money." *Association of Governing Boards*, February 2013.

Holmgren, Richard. "The Real Precipice: Essay on How Technology and New Ways of Teaching Could Upend Colleges' Traditional Models." *Inside Higher Ed*, April 15, 2013.

Laitinen, Amy. "Cracking the Credit Hour." New America Foundation, September 2012.

Laitinen, Amy. "The Curious Birth and Harmful Legacy of the Credit Hour." *The*

Chronicle of Higher Education, January 21, 2013, sec. Commentary.

Levitt, Theodore. "Marketing Myopia." *Harvard Business Review* 38 (August 1960): 24–47. http://hbr.org/2004/07/marketing-myopia/ar/1.

Means, Barbara, Yukie Toyama, Robert Murphy, Marianne Bakia, and Karla Jones. "Evaluation of Evidence-Based Practices in Online Learning: A Meta-Analysis and Review of Online Learning Studies." U.S. Department of Education Office of Planning, Evaluation, and Policy Development Policy and Program Studies Service, September 2010.

Mitrano, Tracy. "What MOOCs Have to Offer Liberal Arts." *Inside Higher Ed*, April 23, 2013.

Mossberg, Walt. "Changing the Economics of Education." *Wall Street Journal*, June 4, 2012.

Nikias, C. L. Max. "Online Education—Hype and Reality," August 27, 2012.

Oblinger, Diana G., and Brian L. Hawkins. "The Myth About Online Course Development." *EDUCAUSE Review*, January 1, 2006.

Parry, Marc. "The Real Revolution Is Openness, Clay Shirky Tells Tech Leaders." The Chronicle of Higher Education. *The Wired Campus*, November 7, 2012.

Rivard, Ry. "Florida Legislation Would Require Colleges to Grant Credit for Some Unaccredited Courses." *Inside Higher Ed*, April 11, 2013.

Schneider, Carol Geary. "Is It Finally Time to Kill the Credit Hour?" *Liberal Education* 98, no. 4 (Fall 2012).

Schur, Richard. "In Defense of the Credit Hour." *The Chronicle of Higher Education*, January 21, 2013, sec. Commentary.

Selingo, Jeffrey. "WHAT PRESIDENTS THINK: A 2013 Survey of Four-Year College Presidents." The Chronicle of Higher Education, 2013.

Snowden, David J., and Mary E. Boone. "A Leader's Framework for Decision Making." *Harvard Business Review* (November 2007).

Young, Jeffrey R. "American Council on Education May Recommend Some Coursera Offerings for College Credit." *The Chronicle of Higher Education*, November 13, 2012, sec. Technology.

Chapter 8: The Rise of the Machines: Big data, learning analytics, and adaptive learning

This chapter is broken into three sections that explore three closely related topics that are not always associated with MOOCs but should be: big data, learning analytics, and adaptive learning. Each of these topics has implications for higher education policy and programs, thus meriting critical review by campus leadership. MOOCs that integrate adaptive learning tools based on big data and learning analytics will likely extend the benefits of these systems, but will also amplify questions and issues related to big data and analytics.

1. Big Data

Big Data is at the heart of modern science and business.[60]
　　　　—Francis X. Diebold, University of Pennsylvania

MOOCs and other online education spaces generate tremendous amounts of data about student behavior, learning styles, and interactions with course material, teachers, and other students. MOOCs also provide data about time spent on particular assignments and engagement in general with the MOOC environment. We can know when students are online and offline, and for how long. Ostensibly, analysis of this data can teach us a great deal about learning. This possibility has people trumpeting *Big Data* as the next big thing.

Big data services are already all around us. Google and

Amazon collect and analyze tremendous amounts of data on their users and customers. Government agencies use big data and analytics to identify patterns of behavior. In general, government and business expect Big Data to help drive decision-making with data and analysis rather than intuition and experience.

With the advent of online learning, higher education is now following the lead of government agencies and for-profit corporations by dipping its toe in the big-data waters. In 2011, Ganesan (Ravi) Ravishanker, Chief Information Officer at Wellesley College, published "Doing Academic Analytics Right: Intelligent Answers to Simple Questions," in the *ECAR Research Bulletin*, published by Educause. Ravishanker argues that "data-driven decision-making is ever more essential." He goes on to say that institutions will do well to encourage systemic interaction with data reports as part of the process of ensuring a return on their investment, and that applying data analytics to institutional learning environments is an opportunity missed on most campuses. With respect to learning management systems and the volumes of interpretable data they represent, Ravishanker encourages campus leaders to question "student and faculty access patterns, how many artifacts are associated with a course, how are students and faculty using the system."[61]

Similarly, in 2012, IBM and *Campus Technology* published "Building a Smarter Campus: How Analytics is Changing the Academic Landscape," reporting that higher ed institutions are increasingly recording the events, activities and assignments of their students. Implementing tools to analyze that data will give decision-makers the ability to predict learning outcomes and better attend

Michael Nanfito

to individual needs: "As the amount of data in higher education is increasing exponentially, data analytics is fast becoming the process-of-choice for colleges and universities that want to improve student learning and campus operations. By turning masses of data into useful and actionable intelligence, higher education institutions are creating smarter campuses—for now and for the future."[62]

Educause, in its 2012 "Study of Analytics in Higher Education," defines analytics as the "use of data, statistical analysis, and explanatory and predictive models to gain insights and act on complex issues."[63] Leaders in higher education are increasingly aware of analytical tools at their disposal. "Predictive tools" help analyze what has happened in a given scenario in order to understand what is likely to happen in the next one; "prescriptive tools" then provide recommendations on how best to respond. Such analytics display patterns in student-generated data and project potential outcomes, allowing for informed decisions based on solid projections rather than on intuition.

MOOCs—and even "traditional" local classroom learning systems—produce massive amounts of data that we may well want to analyze with these tools, in the hopes of improving learning outcomes. Online learning systems, aggregations of data, and the availability of analytics could be converging to rewire the teaching-and-learning circuitry. That potential is driving new vendors to target higher education. A brief review of some emerging players and their products highlights the scope of this emerging academic support industry.

2. Learning Analytics: Three important companies you should know

Apollo Group and Carnegie Learning. In August 2011, the Apollo Group, which runs the University of Phoenix, bought Carnegie Learning, which develops interactive adaptive learning software for math instruction, for $75 million. "Founded by cognitive and computer scientists from Carnegie Mellon University in conjunction with veteran mathematics teachers," Carnegie's website declares, "Carnegie Learning has the courage to not only question the traditional way of teaching math, but re-invent it."

Carnegie Learning entered the higher education market in 2007 after working primarily in middle school and secondary school markets. The company thus has a deep reservoir of content and a decade of experience in developing adaptive learning systems. With its acquisition, Apollo further extends its personalized instruction platform to a broader post-secondary student audience. Apollo hired Mike White away from Yahoo to serve as the Chief Technology Officer for the re-organized Carnegie Learning and assigned more than one hundred technologists to the project. According to White, Apollo sees "adaptive learning as the future. It is about individual learning outcomes."[64]

Pearson and Learning Catalytics. In Spring 2013, Pearson, which has spent more than $1 billion on education companies since 2011 in an effort to extend its reach beyond textbooks and other publications, acquired Learning Catalytics, a learning assessment system created by Harvard University educators Eric Mazur, Brian Lukoff, and Gary King.

The Learning Catalytics system grew out of Mazur's persistent efforts to perfect interactive teaching. That effort is documented in *Peer Instruction: A User's Manual*, which outlines the Peer Instruction method he began developing in the early 1990s and which helped fuel the development and adoption of "classroom clicker" technology. Learning Catalytics' cloud-based software system builds on the clicker model to mine data so as to better "engage students by creating open-ended questions that ask for numerical, algebraic, textual, or graphical responses—or just plain multiple-choice," in the words of the company's website. Instructors use data from the system to send peer interaction directions to students. "Students use any modern web-enabled device they already have—laptop, smartphone, or tablet," and the system mines data generated by their responses to open-ended questions to direct them to peers for interaction and debate.

In "Colleges Mine Data to Tailor Students' Experience" (*The Chronicle of Higher Education*, December 11, 2011), Marc Parry describes how the system is used to direct peer instruction activities in Brian Lukoff's Harvard calculus class: "The software records Ben Falloon's location in the back row and how he answers each practice problem. Come discussion time, it tries to stir up debate by matching students who gave different responses to the most recent question. For Mr. Falloon, the system spits out this prompt: Please discuss your response with Alexis Smith (in front of you) and Emily Kraemer (to your left)."

Instructors receive graphical displays of the responses, recommendations, and results of the interactions. "Advised by the system to interact, they engage in a debate which is the point which gets them arguing—exactly what the matchmaking algorithm intended. Meanwhile, Mr. Lukoff's screen displays a map of how everyone answered the question, data he can use to eavesdrop on specific conversations."

Skeptics, who believe that simply monitoring and cataloging data responses to classroom questions minimizes or even eliminates creativity in the learning environment, consider the modifying of college-level teaching and learning through the use of analytics akin to employing standardized testing in primary and secondary education—with predictable and similar results. Mazur counters that learning analytics systems solve three problems faced by faculty in the contemporary classroom: "One, it selects student discussion groups. Two, it helps instructors manage the pace of classes by automatically figuring out how long to leave questions open so the vast majority of students will have enough time. And three, it pushes beyond the multiple-choice problems typically used with clickers, inviting students to submit open-ended responses, like sketching a function with a mouse or with their finger on the screen of an iPad."[65]

Michael Horner, co-founder and executive director of the Christensen Institute, argues that the ability to harness data generated by analytics frees instructors to focus on working directly with students. Ravishanker also notes in his paper that capturing data about learning activities both in class and online provides faculty and provosts a wealth of information to help evaluate systems currently in place. Horner and others go farther, arguing that analytics will help higher education move away from a factory model of education toward a learning-focused model.

As corporate entities like Pearson partner with the academy, it will be important to review these developments with a critical eye on how they cohere with the strategic needs of your institution. It will be difficult to dismiss out of hand resources that make your own data so readily available, possibly enabling informed development of learning platforms that make sense for this century.

Desire2Learn. Founded in 1999 by John Baker,

Desire2Learn provides cloud-based learning management systems for higher education. In 2012, Desire2Learn entered the learning analytics arms race in earnest with $80 million in financing from New Enterprise Associates and OMERS Ventures. According to an NEA press release, the company is focused on "transforming the way the world learns in a rapidly growing market fueled by the adoption of online and mobile learning tools, digital textbook distribution, and advanced learning analytics."[66]

Desire2Learn has been building toward adding learning analytics to its platform for some time, having developed a team to build a framework of algorithms and predictive models to analyze student learning. The team developed a "risk quadrant" that provides weekly predictive representations of individual learners' progress in a given course. Quadrants display students who are fully engaged and on track towards passing; students who are less engaged but still on track; students who are in danger of withdrawing from the course; and students who are in danger of failing or receiving a poor grade.[67]

The tool begins making data-driven predictions on the first day of a course. Interviewed by Ellis Booker for *Information Week* ("Can Big Data Analytics Boost Graduation Rates?" February 5, 2013), Baker brashly described how dynamic student data, meshed with available historical course data, provides a data framework allowing the system to make predictions of student learning performance with 95 percent accuracy as early as weeks two and three. Desire2Learn launched the learning analytics product as part of an integrated suite of resources called *Desire2Learn Insights*, which the company says can deliver high-performance reports, data visualizations, and predictive analytics to help institutions measure the success of their overall learning environment.

Desire2Learn has taken the analytics toolkit for the classroom that providers like Learning Catalytics have deployed, and implemented it in a cloud-based, intentionally online learning platform wrapped within a familiar learning management system. This has interesting implications for campuses making decisions about MOOCs and other forms of online education.

3. Adaptive Learning

In his article "A History of Teaching Machines" (American Psychologist, September, 1988), Ludy T. Benjamin traced the pedigree and legacy of teaching machines in the U.S: "By the early 1960s, teaching machines were much in the news. National and international conferences were held to discuss the new technology, and popular magazines and scientific journals published news of the emerging research and applications."[68]

Online learning and MOOCs, big data, and analytics, have re-energized a long-standing educational initiative—technology-mediated teaching. Adaptive learning, building on big data and learning analytics, is the latest iteration. Modern adaptive learning includes the implementation of data-driven analytics to help faculty shape the delivery of course materials to adapt to individual abilities. These tools offer personalized learning, mediated by technology. In his essay "Adaptive Learning Could Reshape Higher Ed Instruction" (April 4, 2013, *Inside Higher Ed*), Peter Stokes, executive director of postsecondary innovation in the College of Professional Studies at Northeastern University, describes adaptive learning as "an environment where technology and brain science collaborate with big data to carve out customized pathways through curriculums for individual learners and free up teachers to devote their energies in more productive and scalable ways."[69] (Stokes is also a contributor to the report "LEARNING TO ADAPT: A Case for Accelerating Adaptive Learning in Higher Education," funded by the Bill and Melinda Gates Foundation.)

There is a long history of teaching machines— mechanical, multimedia, and computers—extending back to an 1809 patent for an educational appliance for the teaching of reading. By 1936, there were nearly seven hundred patents for teaching devices. The history of these devices can be traced from the original patented machines of the nineteenth century through the teaching/ testing devices of Sidney Pressey in the 1920s to the more sophisticated teaching machines of Harvard psychologist B.F. Skinner in the 1950s.

Where initial devices were more about testing, late-twentieth-century efforts focused on teaching that enables students to adapt to machine-provided feedback. B.F. Skinner created a mechanical "teaching machine" in the mid-1950s that broke learning into sequenced steps and allowed students to pace themselves as they worked through a series of questions. The steps resembled processes that tutors use to engage students and guide them, via feedback, toward increasingly accurate responses and new knowledge. The machine posed questions and offered new questions only when the student answered correctly; an incorrect answer caused the machine to repeat the question. Skinner's efforts eventually fell out of favor in part because few companies were willing to invest in designing and developing materials for a product with an indeterminate future, but interest in adaptive learning persisted through the latter half of the century with the emergence of affordable personal computers.

Contemporary instructional designers adhere to Skinner's basic tenets, offering adaptive learning tools that present course materials to students who do not move on to subsequent questions until their performance, based on data generated in the adaptive learning process, indicates competency and knowledge. Adaptive learning combines individualized instruction (or rather, something that feels like it to the student), peer interaction, effective and engaging simulations, and applications that dynamically adapt to the learner's abilities.

Because MOOCs and related online and software-mediated learning environments leverage earlier adaptive-learning techniques, campus leadership should consider the value in making historic overview part of their consideration of MOOCs. They might also look for ways to engage private-sector partners in their strategic thinking, particularly since corporate startups are eager to partner with colleges and universities in developing adaptive learning products. In April 2013, Rice University held the first annual Workshop On Personalized Learning, bringing together leaders from higher education and adaptive-learning startup companies to "plot a course to the future of personalized learning" (http://rdls.rice.edu/personalized-learning-workshop). Participants were invited to explore the potential of big data to ensure time and cost efficiencies in the delivery of learning outcomes. Presenters included researchers from Knewton, Carnegie Learning, and Khan Academy as well as faculty and researchers from MIT, Arizona State University, and Duke University.

Meanwhile, the Bill and Melinda Gates Foundation is investing heavily in adaptive learning. The foundation

Michael Nanfito

has solicited proposals from colleges and universities for ten $100,000 grants to help develop new partnerships implementing adaptive learning courses. To encourage participation, the foundation hosted a March 2013 webinar outlining the details of their Adaptive Learning Market Acceleration Program. The session showcased new research indicating that "intelligent" (meaning "digital") tutors are nearly as effective as humans, citing related research by educational psychologist Benjamin Bloom. In 1984, in the journal *Educational Researcher*, Bloom reported that students tutored one-to-one performed two standard deviations better than students taught in conventional lecture courses. Commercial MOOC providers have also touted Bloom's research.

The foundation's strategy is to invest in "market change drivers" that include exemplary implementations of adaptive learning courses combined with research and analysis of learning outcomes in order to accelerate the adoption of adaptive learning in higher education. The Foundation also has formed a loose coalition of leaders from a dozen colleges and two associations to share information about developing and implementing adaptive learning. These schools and this coalition could become a rich laboratory for partnerships between technology vendors and campuses. Participants in the Gates Foundation group include:

American Association of State Colleges and Universities
American Public University System
Arizona State University
Association of Public and Land-Grant Universities
Capella University
Excelsior College
Kaplan University

Kentucky Community and Technical College System
Rio Salado College
Southern New Hampshire University
SUNY Empire State College
University of California at Berkeley
University of Texas at Austin
Western Governors University

The Gates Foundation also commissioned a report from Education Growth Advisors, entitled "Learning To Adapt: A Case for Accelerating Adaptive Learning in Higher Education." (The group also issued a more comprehensive report entitled "Learning to Adapt: Understanding the Adaptive Learning Supplier Landscape.") The report outlines the potential of adaptive learning and how it might help address the "Iron Triangle" of *cost, access* and *quality,* and describes potential adoption paths, opportunities and barriers, solutions, and case studies. It attempts to detail the capabilities of emerging adaptive learning products in an effort to help college leadership make decisions.

The report simplifies campus review of adaptive learning options through analysis of potential benefits of current and emerging providers and products, and includes very brief case studies from a few universities. The document is not unbiased; it reflects the enthusiasm and vision of the Gates Foundation and those who contributed to the narrative. (As its website states, "Education Growth Advisors is affiliated with Education Growth Partners, a Stamford Connecticut-based private equity firm focused exclusively on growth equity investments in education companies in the preK-12, higher education, corporate training, and lifelong learning sectors. Education Growth Partners invests in profitable, innovative, high-potential companies that are seeking capital and expertise to reach scale.") The report opens with three congratulatory scenarios about successful experiences in personalized education, each extolling the potential of adaptive learning systems. The first paragraph of the report is unambiguous: "Welcome to the world of adaptive learning—a more personalized, technology-enabled, and data-driven approach to learning that has the potential to deepen student engagement with learning materials, customize students' pathways through curriculum, and permit instructors to use class time in more focused and productive ways. In this fashion, adaptive learning promises to make a significant contribution to improving retention, measuring student learning, aiding the achievement of better outcomes, and improving pedagogy."[70]

One hears echoes of B.F. Skinner and other, earlier, proponents of now-antiquated "teaching machines" in the report's descriptions of students interacting with course materials in a digital environment. Similar to those earlier claims, we are promised that when "students answer particular questions incorrectly, they may be directed back to appropriate points in the materials to better acquaint themselves with the relevant concepts or facts." It would be difficult to fault the reader for concluding that this is simply the latest iteration of the same old story. It might be tempting to dismiss such reports (and many do) as vehicles for corporate expansion into new and profitable markets. We have survived several generations of enthusiasts and profiteers working to develop technology-mediated education products; it is tempting to say that this one will soon burn itself out as well.

But this time may very well be different. Unlike the earlier mechanical contraptions, which were isolated (and isolating), everyone now has a "teaching machine" in his or her shirt pocket. We are interconnected and interactive in ways not possible before. We have become predisposed to the use of ubiquitous technologies that mediate our information and communication exchanges. On the policy side, there is focused corporate and governmental pressure to innovate in the interest of increasing access to education and improving graduation rates. Foundations are investing in collaborative programs and families are ready for educational alternatives that do not saddle them with life-long debt.

Carnegie Mellon Online Learning Initiative (OLI). More than a decade ago, the late Herbert Simon, Nobel Laureate and professor at Carnegie Mellon University, stated, "Improvement in postsecondary education will require converting teaching from a solo sport to a community-based research activity." Simon's emphatic stance has informed the development and implementation of Carnegie Mellon's Open Learning Initiative (OLI), which began as an effort to integrate digital cognitive tutors and standalone online courses. Beginning in 2002, with funding from the William and Flora Hewlett Foundation, the OLI embarked on a program to develop an online curriculum for "anyone who wants to learn or teach" (Source: OLI website, http://oli.cmu.edu).

In his article, "The Real Precipice," Richard Holmgren, Vice President for Information Services and Planning at Allegheny College, cautions that the "real threat to traditional higher education embraces a more radical vision that removes faculty from the organizational center and uses cognitive science to organize the learning around the learner. Such models exist now."[71] Holmgren goes on to describe how the OLI uses a team approach that includes cognitive scientists, instructional designers, technologists, and faculty disciplinary specialists to design interactive online courses. For a decade or more, the work of the OLI has embodied Peter Stokes' definition of adaptive learning as "an environment where technology and brain science collaborate with big data to carve out customized pathways through curriculums for individual learners." Further, the OLI process is an example of learning analytics at work, as researchers use the data generated from course interactions for persistent course evaluation and re-development as articulated in the goals of the program. The goals of the Carnegie Online Learning Initiative include:

1. Support better learning and instruction with scientifically based, classroom-tested online courses and materials.
2. Share courses and materials openly and freely so that anyone can learn. OLI courses are used by institutions to supplement classroom instruction. They are also designed to support individual independent learners.
3. Develop a community of use, research, and development to allow for the continuous evaluation, improvement, and growth of courses and course materials.

(Source: OLI website, http://oli.cmu.edu)

Holmgren notes that although the OLI is a "proof-of-concept endeavor," it has made compelling advances in blending cognitive science, machine learning, and instructional design. These advances are documented in research from Ithaka S+R that compared face-to-face learning to the hybrid courses rooted in the OLI model. Holmgren notes that according to the study "hybrid courses were at least as effective in promoting student understanding of statistics as traditional courses. Further, students in the hybrid courses learned as much even though they spent significantly less time in learning activities, which echoes earlier work by OLI showing that Carnegie Mellon students learned statistics with OLI in half the time that students in traditional courses did."[72]

Carnegie Mellon has enjoyed a long history of successful integration of cognitive science and technology into learning environments. Prominent among those efforts is the for-profit Carnegie Learning, recently purchased by the Apollo Group. Carnegie Learning's development of digital cognitive tutors to assess students' knowledge and competency and provide a curriculum tailored to individual skill levels was instrumental in crafting the OLI. Embedded cognitive tutors, interactive engagements, and immediate feedback are fundamental components of the OLI. Anya Kamenetz describes the assessment and feedback experience of a learner using the OLI as "what might happen in a classroom under ideal circumstances, with a teacher of infinite patience, undivided attention, and inexhaustible resources of examples and hints" (Kamenetz, Anya, DIY U: Edupunks, Edupreneurs, and the Coming Transformation of Higher Education, New York: Chelsea Green, 2010, 91).

As Holmgren notes, the findings of the Ithaka S+R study are a bit of a milestone. "We can howl in protest, but the question is no longer whether computer-based, intelligent agents can prompt learning of some material at least as well as instructor-focused courses. The question is whether the computer-based version can become even more effective than traditional models, and the implications for

Michael Nanfito

higher education are sobering."

In addition to demonstrable learning outcomes, the assessment and feedback model helps with one of the other distinctive aspects of the OLI: the process is in a persistent state of iterative research, design, assessment, and re-deployment. Cognitive science and instructional design inform initial course development and production, and aggregated data from intentional feedback loops informs subsequent iterations.

In the foreword to *Unlocking The Gates: How And Why Leading Universities Are Opening Up Access To Their Courses* (Taylor Walsh and Ithaka S+R, Princeton University Press, 2011), William G. Bowen describes the benefits and costs of Carnegie Mellon's Online Learning Initiative. Bowen writes that "The OLI is exciting precisely because it may offer the possibility of achieving real productivity gains by substituting well-designed online instruction for the labor-intensive ways in which we still teach many basic courses, including some that lend themselves to less labor-intensive teaching methods." Bowen argues that, despite the costs of programs like the OLI, in the current economic environment "we just can't afford to continue doing business as usual. We have to find ways to do more with less. Resources saved in this way could be redeployed to teach more students or, conceivably, to teach advanced students more effectively." In his view, the OLI has potential in large part because it "lends itself to standard statistical assessments of outcomes—of what was achieved, and at what cost."

The cost is significant. As noted in the Ithaka S+R study, "a new OLI course currently costs about $500,000 to develop—and that figure represents a decline over time, as some of the earlier courses cost over $1 million each."

With significant overhead involved in developing even a single course in this model, it is not surprising that so few courses have been completed. However, the cost does not mean lack of utility or viability. Because Carnegie Mellon is committed to the Open Education Resources movement, all of the OLI courses are available and are being used by educators and students all over the world. According to the Ithaka S+R study, between 2006 and 2010 there were 18,516 student registrations for the Academic Version and—significantly—73,062 registrations for the open (and free) courses representing global use in 214 countries. Although it would be financially impossible for a lone institution to adopt *and sustain* the grant-funded OLI methodology to develop and deliver adaptive learning courses, it is conceivable that the model has potential in the distributed, unbundled model of MOOCs.

The "New Way College" Model. In his "Precipice" article in *Inside Higher Ed*, Holmgren offers a hypothetical scenario for just how an alternative model integrating the OLI, existing universities, and corporate interests might work. In this scenario, a university that is already committed to, and active in, online competency-based credentialing would partner with a provider similar to the OLI to create a fictional online college (call it "New Way College") within the larger host institution. New Way College provides a basic curriculum of hybrid courses with no more than twenty students per course, enabling students to earn an associate degree at significant cost savings.

Holmgren's financial model for New Way College is compelling: Students pay $400 for a four-credit course, and sixteen courses are required for an associate degree. Student cost for the degree would be $6,400, and students qualifying for the maximum Pell grant could have their degree fully underwritten by the federal government. For local organizations, suppose New Way partnered with a public library to offer a course for 15 students and the course is staffed by volunteers from a literacy program. In this example, the public library collects $1800, which would be a boon for local libraries beset by budget cuts, while the curriculum provider and the host university each collect $600, and the testing/proctor firm would receive $3000. Considered at the scale of the university and corporate partners, even a modest program of 30 courses with average enrollment of 10,000 students would generate $84 million to be divided among the curriculum provider, host university, and testing service. Another $36 million would be split among local hosts.

"By unbundling the learning experience—separating local support, course design, delivery, assessment, administrative support, and advising—the NWC model achieves superior outcomes at lower cost, at least when outcomes are measured by exam or other task performance. Local organization and student support is provided by entities with deep roots in their communities, missions aligned with the educational endeavor, existing meeting spaces that are often underutilized and could readily be used to house weekly class meetings, access to volunteer or relatively low-cost tutors to provide student support, and budget constraints that create incentives to leverage these resources to market and support classes for their communities," Holmgren writes. Such a model could well revitalize local host organizations looking for renewed revenue in harsh economic times. Such disruptive innovation could also wreak financial havoc with local colleges competing in the same market in more traditional fashion.

It is easy to imagine organizations like the Saylor Foundation and StraighterLine developing such a model. A surplus of post-doc Ph.Ds with no realistic hope of securing a traditional tenure-track position provide an abundant labor force for local host organizations. The enthusiasm and prior investment of venture capital players in this market suggests that such a model may well be highly attractive to them.

There are real limitations to the OLI model, including significant overhead cost. Further, the model seems to be restricted to courses like mathematics and statistics, the humanities being completely unrepresented to date. These limitations notwithstanding, the extensibility of the program shows promise; the OLI's iterative model of persistent research, design, and development making use of data generated by student interaction with material will likely be integrated into, and influence, MOOCs and other online platforms. Such integration, in fact, is already under way.

Platforms and Publishers: delivering on adaptive learning. The report "Learning To Adapt" makes an important distinction between adaptive learning "platforms" and course content "publishers." To date, campuses have generally had choices between vendors offering platforms with adaptive learning authoring tools and publishers providing course content with delivery models that try to incorporate adaptive learning.

Platform providers sell infrastructure and software for developing adaptive learning models. Examples include aNewSpring, Cerego, CogBooks, Knewton, LoudCloud, and Smart Sparrow. Publishers active in this market

　　　　　Michael Nanfito

include traditional firms eager to capitalize on emerging commercial opportunities—such companies as Cengage, Jones & Bartlett Learning, Macmillan, McGraw-Hill, Pearson, and Wiley. Emerging digital-only publishing include Adapt Courseware and the Open Learning Initiative.

For now, the most successful providers working in the adaptive learning market may be those traditional publishers with the wherewithal to leverage existing content in new ways while negotiating productive partnerships with emerging *platform* providers. These partnerships are worth monitoring as they provide vendors a powerful vehicle to sell innovative educational resources to higher education and to insert themselves into the dialogue about the future of educational content. As Mitchel Stevens of Stanford University has noted, who gets a seat at that table is still up for grabs. Campus leaders would do well to shoulder their way in and not wait for an invitation to help shape the future.[73]

Of new partnerships that have emerged, that between publisher Pearson and platform provider Knewton appears to have gained the most significant traction. Pearson is busily amassing a substantial portfolio of education companies through both purchases and partnerships. In addition to acquiring Learning Catalytics, for example, they have partnered with a rising startup called Knewton.

Founded by former Kaplan executive Jose Ferreira, Knewton is an adaptive learning infrastructure platform provider. Expanding on earlier successes of efforts like Carnegie Mellon's Online Learning Initiative, the Knewton infrastructure "makes it possible for anyone to build the world's most powerful adaptive learning applications. Knewton technology consolidates data science, statistics, psychometrics, content graphing, machine learning, tagging, and infrastructure in one place in order to enable personalization at massive scale" (Source: http://www.knewton.com).

Knewton builds on the past decade of work in big data and learning analytics. Ferreira is adamant about the power of mining big data and marrying analytics to digital course content in order to turn the traditional classroom on its head, thereby freeing instructors to manage their time in new ways. Ferreira and his team are aggressively pursuing the potential of big data and analytics. In an interview with Marc Parry of the *Chronicle of Higher Ed* ("A Conversation With 2 Developers of Personalized-Learning Software," *The Chronicle of Higher Education*, July 18, 2012), Ferreira noted the disparity in the scope of data available from services like Google and the data available from a student engaging with digital course materials: "You do a search for Google; Google gets about 10 data points. They get, by our standards, a very small amount of data compared to what we get per user per day. If they can produce that kind of personalization and that kind of business, based off the small amount of data they get, imagine what we can do in education," he says. Ferreira and the Knewton team have developed a platform to extract a great deal of data from the user experience: "Knewton's capturing in the hundreds of thousands of data per user per day. We're capturing what you're getting right, what you're getting wrong, what answers you're falling for if you get something wrong, what concepts are in that answer choice that you're falling for. We're also capturing when you log into the system; how much you do; what tasks you do; what you don't do; what was recommended that you do that you didn't do, and vice versa."[74]

All of this data extraction results in predictions about learning outcomes followed by prescriptions for follow-up actions for each student. Applying the system's learning analytics to the data generated by student interactions leads to "the perfect sentence, or perfect clip, or perfect problem for you at any one time, based on what you're the weakest at, and what's most important, and how you learn it best." As part of this effort, Knewton is launching what it calls "learning modality adaptivity," a feature that will discern what and how much to show each student each day. The module is intended to understand how students learn best and when to present content appropriate to learning abilities and demonstrated progress. According to Ferreira, his system will "figure out things like, you learn math best with a video clip, or you learn science best with games instead of text, or in addition to text—and we can figure out what the optimal ratio is for you. We can figure out things like, you learn math best in the morning, and verbal concepts best in the evening, on average. Maybe you learn math best between 8:32 and 9:14. If so, we'll know it. It means when you show up in the morning to do some practice, we're going to try to feed you math, and if you show up in the evening, we'll try to feed you more verbal, because that's when you're most receptive to those subject matters."[75]

Adaptive learning systems do not stop with individual learners. The power of such programs lies in the interconnectivity of all data streams of all students in the course. Predictions and prescriptive actions are personalized for each student, with the learning trajectories of different students divergent by design. The system decides which course modules will be presented to each student, and when, based on data mining and analytics. In this regard, Knewton is representative of the marriage of big data, learning analytics, and personalized adaptive learning that fosters such potentially disruptive models as self-paced learning and flipped classrooms. By measuring productivity and progress, Knewton's and other adaptive learning systems will recommend different times of the day for different students to "crack the book." This blows up the standardized classroom model governed by the calendar and the clock, and gestures toward a hybridized, self-paced learning model.

Adaptive learning models may encourage consideration of alternatives to credentialing that are currently based on seat time and the credit hour. They may be attractive to institutions eager for solutions to problems of access to college, cost containment, and degree completion rates. Emerging partnerships and collaborations between corporations and startups that likely would have been competitors just a few years ago may fuel additional disruptive (or distracting) models.

Knewton's partnership with Pearson allows it to leverage pre-existing contractual relationships with higher education institutions to deliver course content in a new way. The digital content of every Pearson textbook must now be "tagged" with metadata that powers the Knewton analytics system. Pearson can now use the Knewton model to re-power existing online reading and mathematics courses. With significant shares of the higher education textbook and digital book markets, the deal gives Knewton a boost as it markets to institutions. Perhaps most significantly, Knewton now has access to pre-existing student data captured in the Pearson machine. The infusion

Michael Nanfito

of this comparative data will increase the accuracy of the Knewton system.

All of this is relevant to the consideration of MOOCs and online learning vendors. Daphne Koller, co-founder of Coursera, speaks of the analytical strengths of MOOCs, extolling their adaptive pedagogy. "We can now do the kind of rapid evolution in education that is common at companies like Google, which 'A/B test' their ad positions and user interface elements for effectiveness," she has said. "These websites evolve in a matter of days or weeks rather than years" (Booker, Ellis. "Can Big Data Analytics Boost Graduation Rates?" *Information Week*, February 5, 2013).

Many will object to the use of data mining, learning analytics, and other methodologies that inform website advertising in the development of academic learning environments. Even some MOOC proprietors are dubious. Mike Feerick, CEO of Advance Learning Interactive Systems Online (ALISON), which provides interactive multimedia courseware for certification and standards-based learning, acknowledges the importance of data analytics while also asserting that expecting such tools to solve education's problems is simply wrong. Feerick is just as adamant that talented and dedicated teachers who make effective use of these emerging tools are the key to pedagogical success as Koller and Ferreira are about the promise of data mining and analytics.[76]

Media coverage of this issue highlights the technologies that these adaptive learning entrepreneurs promote, leading many to assume that they seek to supplant educators with software. Along with the persistent drumbeat coming out of these startups, the coverage inspires observations from scholars like Evgeny Morozov, who describes misplaced faith in technology as a "dangerous ideology." In his article "The Perils of Perfection" (*New York Times*, March 2, 2013), Morozov labels this ideology "solutionism: an intellectual pathology that recognizes problems as problems based on just one criterion: whether they are 'solvable' with a nice and clean technological solution at our disposal." He explains his ideas more fully in his book, *To Save Everything, Click Here: The Folly of Technological Solutionism*. Morozov raises important questions about the expectations our culture holds out for technological solutions to cultural and social problems. He specifically questions the impact of "nice and clean" big data solutions on our ability to negotiate the messy business of living and learning. Morozov argues that, in the effort to cleanse our social and cultural institutions of that messiness—"from education to publishing and from music to transportation" —in the name of mere efficiency is to lose the benefit of the struggle and decision-making that contribute to maturity. Morozov cites Sartre, who "celebrated the anguish of decision as a hallmark of responsibility," and notes that celebrating the value of such inefficiency and struggle "has no place in Silicon Valley."

Indeed, there is undeniable value in inefficiency and imperfection. We learn from our mistakes and we do well to foster spaces where we can mess up and gain insights from the process. Proponents of adaptive learning are confident that the digital spaces they are creating are just that—spaces where we learn from our mistakes. At issue for higher education is the extent to which we identify and implement big data and adaptive learning solutions. Morozov's concerns notwithstanding, these resources will be part of whatever MOOCs and learning management systems colleges and universities put in place. We must ensure

Michael Nanfito

that we understand how to make the best use of these tools as *supplements* to the established value and success of educators. We need to listen to the cautionary tales of those like Morozov to understand the reasonable limits of such potentially invasive technologies. Campus leaders and stakeholders across all sectors of higher education and from all sorts of institutions need to fully understand the implications of these proposed solutions, insert appropriate checks and balances, and ensure continued appreciation for the necessarily awkward messiness of learning.

Ethical Implications of Big Data, Analytics, and Adaptive Learning. In addition to the concerns of Morozov and others about surrendering the benefits of traditional, albeit imperfect, spaces to the sanitized environments of adaptive learning, there are ethical issues regarding the use of data collected via MOOCs and other online learning environments. The expansive dimensions of big data will uncover new obligations on the part of the institution to act in the interest of the student once the institution "knows" and can predict something about that student's performance. Accumulating and aggregating analyses of big data, by design, results in predictions about performance and may raise privacy concerns. Reviewing such analyses will require decisions regarding appropriate allocation of such institutional resources as faculty, curricular design, and staff support. An institution will need to determine whether there are reporting and/or disclosure issues. Policies may need to be drafted about informing students and faculty about the type, nature, and scope of data being collected about them. Existing policies will need to be reviewed to understand whether they address big data issues.

The May 6, 2013, edition of *EDUCAUSE Review* included an article by James Willis, John Campbell, and Matthew Pistilli, entitled "Ethics, Big Data, and Analytics: A Model for Application," which offers an in-depth analysis of the implications of big data in higher education. With respect to emerging big data opportunities and questions, the authors enjoin campus leaders to "understand the dynamic nature of academic success and retention, provide an environment for open dialogue, and develop practices and policies to address these issues."[77] They outline the ethical issues involved in implementing big data solutions on campus and offer prescriptive guidelines for policy development.

As part of their research, the authors reviewed the outcomes of Purdue University's *Signals* project, which uses big data and analytics to detect "early warning signs and provides intervention to students who may not be performing to the best of their abilities before they reach a critical point" (source: www.itap.purdue.edu/studio// signals/). The authors conclude that the Signals project has improved retention and graduation rates, illuminating an interesting set of decisions about resource allocation. They credit feedback from the big data component of the Signals project for increasing student success: "Students who are less prepared for college—as measured solely by standardized test score—are retained by and graduated from Purdue at higher rates than their better-prepared peers after having one or more courses in which Signals was used." Knowing that the mediating impact of data analytics improves academic performance of students who are less well prepared for college raises questions about allocation of resources and the accountability of the institution. "With access to these predictive formulas, faculty

Michael Nanfito

members, students, and institutions must confront their responsibilities related to academic success and retention, elevating these key issues from a 'general awareness' to a quantified value." Inserting big data and adaptive learning systems into MOOCs will likely enhance their potential for positive mediation of student learning outcomes. It will also amplify the impact and scope of these issues.

Francis Diebold is the Paul F. and Warren S. Miller Professor of Economics in the School of Arts and Sciences at the University of Pennsylvania. He is also Professor of Finance and Statistics in the Wharton School University of Pennsylvania. Diebold asserts that big data is "not merely taking us to bigger traditional places. Rather, it's taking us to wildly new places, unimaginable only a short time ago." If so, various current institutional policies are inadequate. To help with policy review and revision, Willis, Campbell, and Pistilli offer a set of questions that help inform implementation of big data in campus learning systems. They are worth sharing here:

- Does the college inform students that their academic behaviors are tracked?

- What and how much information should be provided to the student?

- What and how much information does the institution give faculty members?

- Does the institution provide a calculated probability of academic success or just a classification of success (e.g., above average, average, below average)?

- What guidelines are provided to faculty regarding the use of the student data?

- Should the faculty member contact students directly?

- Will the data influence perceptions of the student and the grading of assignments?

- What amount of resources should the institution invest in students who are unlikely to succeed in a course?

- What obligation does the student have to seek assistance?

Building on the research and related issues, the authors propose three specific responsibilities institutions must embrace in order to ensure academic success for faculty and students in an era of massive data aggregation in online adaptive learning environments in this new era:

- The institution is responsible for developing, refining, and using the massive amount of data it collects to improve student success and retention, as well as for providing the tools and information necessary to promote student academic success and retention.

- The institution is responsible for providing students and faculty members with the training and support necessary to use the tools in the most effective manner. It further is responsible for providing students with excellent instructional opportunities, student advising, and a supportive learning environment, as well as for providing faculty members with tools that allow them to deliver timely feedback to students on their progress within their courses.

- The institution is responsible for providing a campus

climate that is both attractive and engaging and that enhances the likelihood that students will connect with faculty and other students, and for recognizing and rewarding faculty and staff who are committed to student academic success and retention.

Institutions will need to determine their capacity to manage the implications of big data. Commercial entry and expansion into the learning analytics and adaptive learning market is increasing dramatically and is already informing the development of MOOCs. That increase adds to the array of issues senior leadership in higher education must consider as part of the strategic integration of pedagogy and technology in the context of the campus mission.

Planning Questions.

The authors of "Ethics, Big Data, and Analytics: A Model for Application," suggest specific questions to address when considering adoption and implementation of big data on campus:

1. What is the role of big data in education?
2. How can big data enrich the student experience?
3. Will the use of big data increase retention?
4. To what extent can big data contribute to successful outcomes?

Further, as you consider the implications of learning analytics at your institution, additional questions to ask include:

5. Are you already using data analytics?
6. Do you have an organizational culture supporting the use of data analytics for decision-making?
7. Does your institution have the organizational adaptability to implement analytics in the culture?
8. Does your institution currently have the

organizational capacity and skill sets to make good use of data analytics?

9. Are you aware of and have you made use of the ECAR Analytics Maturity Index available from Educause?

10. Have you reviewed your institution's strategic plan to identify issues that would benefit from analytics?

11. Do you view analytics as strategic investment or additional cost?

Chapter 8 Endnotes

60. Diebold, "A Personal Perspective on the Origin(s) and Development of 'Big Data': The Phenomenon, the Term, and the Discipline."

61. Ravishanker, "Doing Academic Analytics Right: Intelligent Answers to Simple Questions."

62. IBM, "Building a Smarter Campus- How Analytics Is Changing the Academic Landscape."

63. Bichsel, "Analytics in Higher Education: Benefits, Barriers, Progress, and Recommendations."

64. Keller, "Apollo to Buy Adaptive-Learning Company for $75-Million."

65. Parry, "Colleges Mine Data to Tailor Students' Experience."

66. "Desire2Learn Raises $80 Million in Financing Round from NEA and OMERS Ventures."

67. Booker, "Can Big Data Analytics Boost Graduation Rates?".

68. Benjamin, "A History of Teaching Machines."

69. Stokes, "Adaptive Learning Could Reshape Higher Ed Instruction (essay)."

70. NEWMAN, STOKES, and BRYANT, "LEARNING TO ADAPT: A Case for Accelerating Adaptive Learning in Higher Education."

71. Holmgren, "The Real Precipice."

72. Ibid.

73. Kolowich, "The New Intelligence."

74. Parry, "A Conversation With 2 Developers of Personalized-Learning Software."

75. Ibid.

76. Booker, "Can Big Data Analytics Boost Graduation Rates?".

77. Willis, Campbell, and Pistilli, "Ethics, Big Data, and Analytics: A Model for Application."

Michael Nanfito

Chapter 8: The Rise of the Machines: Big data, learning analytics, and adaptive learning - Recommended Readings

Benjamin, Ludy T. "A History of Teaching Machines." *American Psychologist* 43, no. 9 (September 1988): 703–712.

Booker, Ellis. "Can Big Data Analytics Boost Graduation Rates?" *Information Week*, February 5, 2013.

Diebold, Francis X. "A Personal Perspective on the Origin(s) and Development of 'Big Data': The Phenomenon, the Term, and the Discipline." University of Pennsylvania, November 26, 2012.

Education Growth Advisors. "Learning To Adapt: Understanding The Adaptive Learning Supplier Landscape," April 2013.

Fain, Paul. "Gates Foundation Helps Colleges Keep Tabs on Adaptive Learning Technology." *Inside Higher Ed*, April 4, 2013.

Fischman, Josh. "Popular Pearson Courseware Revamps by Offering 'Adaptive Learning'." The Chronicle of Higher Education. *The Wired Campus*, November 1, 2011.

———. "The Rise of Teaching Machines." *The Chronicle of Higher Education*, May 8, 2011, sec. The Digital Campus 2011.

Holmgren, Richard. "The Real Precipice: Essay on How Technology and New Ways of Teaching Could Upend Colleges' Traditional Models." *Inside Higher Ed*, April 15, 2013.

Kolowich, Steve. "Arizona St. and Knewton's Grand Experiment with Adaptive Learning." *Inside Higher Ed*, January 25, 2013.

Lohr, Steve. "How Big Data Became So Big - Unboxed." *The New York Times*, August 11, 2012, sec. Business Day.

McLemee, Scott. "Review of Matthew L. Jockers, 'Macroanalysis: Digital Methods & Literary History'." *Inside Higher Ed*, May 1, 2013.

McRae, Philip. "Rebirth of the Teaching Machine through the Seduction of Data Analytics: This Time It's Personal." *Philip McRae, Ph.D.*, April 4, 2013.

New, Jake. "Online-Learning Portal Allows Educators to Create Adaptive Content." The Chronicle of Higher Education. *The Wired Campus*, April 17, 2013.

———. "Pearson Acquires Learning Catalytics, a Cloud-Based Assessment System." The Chronicle of Higher Education. *The Wired Campus*, April 22, 2013.

Parry, Marc. "A Conversation With 2 Developers of Personalized-Learning Software." *The Chronicle of Higher Education*, July 18, 2012, sec. Technology.

———. "Colleges Mine Data to Tailor Students' Experience." *The Chronicle of Higher Education*, December 11, 2011.

Ravishanker, Ganesan (Ravi). "Doing Academic Analytics Right: Intelligent Answers to Simple Questions." *ECAR Research Bulletin* 2 (2011).

Stokes, Peter. "Adaptive Learning Could Reshape Higher Ed Instruction (essay)." *Inside Higher Ed*, April 4, 2013.

"The First Annual Rice University Workshop On Personalized Learning." *Center for Digital Learning and Scholarship (RDLS)*, April 22, 2013. http://rdls.rice.edu/personalized-learning-workshop.

Walsh, Taylor, and Ithaka S+R. "Unlocking The Gates: How And Why Leading Universities Are Opening Up Access To Their Courses." PRINCETON UNIVERSITY PRESS, 2011.

Warner, John. "We Don't Need No Adaptive Learning | Inside Higher Ed." *Inside Higher Ed*, April 4, 2013.

Watters, Audrey. "Top Ed-Tech Trends of 2012: Data and Learning Analytics." *Inside Higher Ed*, December 20, 2012.

Willis, James E., John P. Campbell, and Matthew D. Pistilli. "Ethics, Big Data, and Analytics: A Model for Application." *EDUCAUSE Review*, May 6, 2013.

Chapter 9: CONCLUSION: Think Strategically— Not Defensively

"Most time is invested in doing the routine work that maintains the status quo and keeps us safe, recognizing of course that safety is defined very differently by different people. Until we are willing to let go of some of that routine but seemingly essential work, there won't be enough time to drive change . . . More specifically, the problem may be that you hold two conflicting desires, the desire for change and the desire for stability or safety, which is typically grounded in some unarticulated and unexamined assumption about what safety is and means. Those two impulses (probably more than two but we simplify for exposition) have led to a stable equilibrium. We can push against it, but when we get tired of pushing, the most likely (almost certain) outcome is a return to equilibrium unless we have changed the underlying assumptions. So, the real work of change is uncovering and challenging those assumptions."

—Richard Holmgren, Allegheny College

The growth of online learning options continues to proliferate—for good reason. With a great deal of perceived opportunity in such ventures, significant corporate investment is flowing into MOOCs, big data, learning analytics, and adaptive learning products and services, reflecting corporate conviction that profit is to be made there. Heavy corporate investment will direct the development of learning platforms being made available to your campus, your faculty, and your students. At the moment, development of these resources is nascent; thus you have an opportunity, as a steward of the academic mission, to ensure that the interests of your constituencies are represented during online learning's development phase.

We have the opportunity and obligation to heed Holmgren's advice to uncover and challenge our assumptions so as to determine how MOOCs and online learning make sense for higher education, decide where they fit in the mission of the college or university, and recognize that they are here to stay in one form or another. Leadership in higher education must participate in the development and dialogue of MOOCs, actively assess how they fit in the broader context of twenty-first-century education, and determine how such resources can be made a meaningful part of the institution's overall mission and strategy.

The flurry of startups that prompted Thomas Friedman to declare "a college education revolution" notwithstanding, MOOCs are a node in the trajectory of educational technology development that stretches back decades. And while proponents cite MOOCs as a solution to the current crises in higher education, and detractors view them as destroyers of institutions delivering an invaluable educational experience, the truth lies somewhere between. Reaction on both sides has been disproportionate. Yet questions raised remain pertinent: What is the future of academic credit in light of the changes wrought by emerging online learning? How will institutions evaluate MOOC credits and open badges on the transcripts of applicants? What are the true costs of MOOCs? Are they financially sustainable? How will we balance support for existing programs while funding MOOCs on the basis of their potential? What exactly is the value of online education and adaptive learning to institutions and students?

Michael Nanfito

MOOCs have been built upon previous, less-publicized iterations in online learning and open educational resources, and thus are an incremental step forward in the movement toward delivering education online. As previously noted, Jack Wilson, president emeritus of the University of Massachusetts, remarked "They're certainly not the first movers; they're not even the fast followers." The open education opportunity that characterizes these emergent forms is inherently more democratic and inclusive. In order for MOOCs and other online education initiatives to live up to their potential, the efforts of colleges and universities (and organizations and associations) not on the roster of usual suspects must be acknowledged and supported. Higher education community members must grapple with their relationship to commercial interests and find ways to partner with them in a collaborative manner rather than negotiate with them as mere consumers.

As investments proliferate, MOOCs will continue to dominate education news and the (often contradictory) daily commentary will have us believe that they are the solution to every challenge facing colleges or universities. Constant competing news briefs posit that MOOCs will variously lower (or raise) the cost of education, increase (or diminish) revenue, shorten time to graduation or create a confusing swirl of conflicting credential models, solve the classroom shortage problem, and provide expansive access to elite faculty while simultaneously diminishing the value of—and need for—faculty in general.

For campus leadership responsible for carrying through on institutional obligation, it is vital to cut through the fog of rhetoric. Focus on strategies that advance the strategic mission. Analyze reports and review them with staff and colleagues in the context of your stated strategic plan and existing consortial relationships. Challenge your peers and partners to better articulate their rationale for adopting or eschewing emerging opportunities. Require everyone to consider the implications of MOOCs not as a standalone construct but in the larger context of the development of all open and online education resources. If it is accurate to say that a majority of presidents believe that online education supports the institutional mission, provides vehicles to reach learners, and increases enrollment and revenue, it is critical to articulate how and why these developments will come to fruition. Faculty and staff will need to appreciate the connections between MOOCS, online and adaptive learning, and the educational job of the institution.

Given conflicting op-ed pieces and the scope of publicly advertised campus dissension on these issues, it is clear that the opportunity for clarity and confirmation remains wide open. Identify expectations and synch them with articulated institutional needs. Assess your organizational structure and its capacity to meet these expectations in a practical, programmatic manner. Educate the institution as a whole on the meaning, implications, costs, and compromises to be expected in implementing MOOCs, online learning, and open educational resources. Be inclusive, engaging faculty, staff, and students in this effort. Understand when to reach out to others for as unbiased a review as is possible. To reiterate the advice of Kenneth Hartman (former president of Drexel eLearning at Drexel University), "it requires the thoughtful use of both internal and external resources, including . . . the careful use of third-party vendors and consultants to properly assess your institution's market niche." Without knowing the "why," it

Michael Nanfito

makes no sense to press too far down the path toward the "how."

We know we have too few colleges and universities, and too many aspiring students, for our current system to accommodate the unmet need. We continue to clamor for an educated populace with the analytical skills that college education provides, yet we ask too much of the existing education infrastructure to deliver on our expectations. Various iterations of online learning have the potential to make an emerging form of higher education available to those who are excluded because of space limitations or inability to pay. MOOCs have the potential to address this burgeoning challenge. We all (trustees, presidents, senior administration, faculty, staff, and students) should be able to pose and respond to such questions as "How does this opportunity synch with our institutional mission?" "What opportunity does this represent?" "How will we organize to avail ourselves of this opportunity?" "What will we miss if we fail to execute on this in a responsible manner?" "What is my responsibility?"

The questions regarding MOOCs are real, as is the urgency felt in many quarters. But the aggregate of questions pressing for attention are not entirely about MOOCs, which are not in and of themselves the massive opportunity or threat that many have made them out to be. Rather, their emergence at this time has helped raise (or resurrect) questions that deserve attention, responses, and action.

The rise of MOOCs has engendered or deepened questions about measuring academic competency, scholarship and authorship in networked collaborative environments, the role of faculty and students, and the business of higher education. No campus is an island when it comes to policy, funding, financial aid, or demographics. Every campus in every sector of higher education is a stakeholder in the policy decisions about credit, credentialing, and funding. Even if your campus never hosts a MOOC or offers an online learning program leading to a degree, your institution will not escape the widespread influence of MOOCs and online learning.

The Seduction and the Allure. The potential of technology seduces even as it threatens and challenges. The ability to extend institutional reach and brand, to enhance learning and enrich teaching, are all within reach. We see the possibilities even as new and recurring questions loom large.

Innovations in education and technology have repeatedly proven to be neither harbingers of doom nor panaceas. However, some of the most recent innovations and collaborations enabling MOOCs raise unprecedented questions engendering conversations about organization, delivery, authentication, and credentialing of the higher education experience as we slide inexorably towards the midpoint of the twenty-first century. The questions and conversations are simultaneously exciting and overwhelming. Pleas to simply "get on with it" are simplistic. We need first to understand the connective tissue between the component parts of the issues, applying self-reflection and critical analysis to our institution's unique situation. In the final analysis, the MOOC debate is not just about MOOCs.

The online learning threat/opportunity presses campus leaders to participate in the development of strategic policy that will influence the shape of higher education for the coming century. The variables are daunting; you will need

Michael Nanfito

to isolate them in order to define the problem statement and map a viable path forward. Identify and separate the simple from the complicated, the complex from the chaotic. Understand where these component parts lie in the continuum. Identify and make use of knowledge management and decision-making tools at your disposal. Participate in policy development.

Online learning is here to stay. The traditional profile of educators and learners, the shape of the college and university, and the nature of policy development are undergoing internal and external analysis and, to some extent, reshaping. The resulting new policies and legislation will inevitably impact all of higher education.

In reality, this is nothing new; others have confronted and faced similar challenges in the past. Over a century ago, leaders wrestled with an American educational system that was fractured, provincial, and occasionally idiosyncratic. Making the most of the tools and resources available to them, they developed an acceptable approach to standardizing the college and university experience for faculty and student alike. That persistent process has been in play ever since. Just as previous generations contributed the values, enthusiasms, and expectations of their time to the business of educating, it is our opportunity at this time to outline the issues and prepare the solutions that carry us forward into the next century.

Printed in Great Britain
by Amazon.co.uk, Ltd.,
Marston Gate.